Swim against
the Current

For Lino —

Swim against the Current

Even a Dead Fish Can Go with the Flow

JIM HIGHTOWER
with SUSAN DeMARCO

WILEY

John Wiley & Sons, Inc.

Published by John Wiley & Sons, Inc., Hoboken, New Jersey
Published simultaneously in Canada

For general information about our other products and services, please contact our Customer Care Department within the United States at (800) 762-2974, outside the United States at (317) 572-3993 or fax (317) 572-4002.

Wiley also publishes its books in a variety of electronic formats. Some content that appears in print may not be available in electronic books. For more information about Wiley products, visit our web site at www.wiley.com.

Library of Congress Cataloging-in-Publication Data:

Hightower, Jim, date.
   Swim against the current : even a dead fish can go with the flow / Jim Hightower
with Susan DeMarco.
      p.   cm.
   Includes index.
   ISBN 978-0-470-12151-1 (cloth)
1. Business and politics—United States. 2. Corporate power—United States.
3. Democracy—United States. 4. United States—Politics and government.
5. American wit and humor. I. DeMarco, Susan. II. Title
   JK467.H54   2008
   322'.30973—dc22   2007027348

Printed in the United States of America

10   9   8   7   6   4   3   2   1

To Molly Ivins, for all she did
and all she was

"The people have the power
The power to dream
To rule
To wrestle the world from fools."

—Patti Smith

Contents

Acknowledgments

For first-rate research, artful use of the Internet, good ideas, and personable dealings with all of the people involved with this book—thank you, Laura Ehrlich. For six years (and three books), Laura has handled everything from communications to production work, keeping our little shop (Saddle-Burr Productions) running smoothly—at least, when I don't screw things up.

Thanks, too, to Marva Mouser in our office, who helped lift the research load, and to Melody Byrd, who has the unenviable task of coordinating the book-tour schedule.

Rafe Sagalyn is the sort of agent writers need—calm in the storm, yet willing to kick up a storm when one is necessary. Thanks for bringing our book to print. And thanks, too, for introducing DeMarco and me to Eric Nelson and all the good folks who make John Wiley & Sons such a welcoming place for maverick voices like ours.

Finally, a special thank-you to the mavericks whose stories we tell here. You activists, entrepreneurs, politicos, organizers, doctors, environmentalists, religious leaders, unionists, reformers, farmers, scientists, and other odd bedfellows—creative souls all—are a shining light to a brighter future for all of us. Thanks for being such a positive force in an often negative world.

Introduction

"You don't have a soul. You are a soul. You have a body."

—C. S. Lewis

Rambling down the dusty road of life, DeMarco and I have picked up a few useful bits of advice, which we now pass along for guidance in your own journeys (no need to thank us; happy to be of assistance):

- Never eat at a café featuring "Bargain kebabs!"
- Never hit a man with glasses; hit him with something much heavier.
- Never get into a drinking contest with a tattooed woman called "Tanker."

Okay, so we have also picked up a few serious words of wisdom over the years. We've found in them a path that makes life more interesting and much richer than it otherwise would be. Here's a small set of these maxims, all related, all culturally charged, and all worthy of being embraced as touchstones of a new progressive revival to lift us from the corporate doldrums that have stalled our country's revolutionary drive:

Question authority.

Question their answers.

Trust your values.

Stand up for your beliefs.

Take risks.

Invite change.

Seek alternatives.

Break away.

Make a difference.

Last year, I got this e-mail from a woman named Linda:

> I have a decent job and do it well, but I'm constantly thinking I'm wasting my time. I want to begin doing something useful to contribute to changing things, at least becoming a cog in the wheel that's on the right vehicle. Any suggestions?

First, Linda, you are not alone. So many people yearn to break away but can't express it so succinctly. Second, in ways both small and large, it's quite possible for each of us to make the break, whether we're young and just starting out, or we're older and in search of another path.

We've written this book to give people a sense of the various possibilities for escaping the corporate tentacles. The Powers That Be don't want you even thinking that this is achievable. But, as a friend of ours says, "Those who say it can't be done should not interrupt those who are doing it."

In our many travels throughout this great country, DeMarco and I have come across all sorts of commonsense folks who're choosing to buck the system . . . and succeeding. They are not Einsteins, not heirs to a Rockefeller fortune, not people who just got lucky. They simply are regular Americans who decided to reject the prescribed rules and exit the corporate interstate. They're showing us new paths toward richer lives and—(dare we say it?)—happiness.

Our book will introduce you to some of these people, tell their stories, and connect you to individuals and groups that can help *you* navigate a different course. These are stories of people in business, politics, and other pursuits who are defining success for themselves, taking charge, living their values, doing good, and doing well. They are doing precisely what the elites want you to believe can't be done: changing their lives . . . and making a difference.

> "Be yourself; everyone else is already taken."
>
> —Oscar Wilde

The institutions of power use everything from the lure of money to the blinders of conventional wisdom to keep us hitched to their plows, but the wonderful thing about Americans is that we have a healthy rebellious streak and the freedom to make choices. DeMarco and I urge everyone to tap into his or her maverick potential, but we hope that young people (teens and young adults) especially will question the rigid track that the system puts them on, insisting that it is *the only way* to live your life.

It's our belief that the kind of rebels you'll read about in this book are the great hope and the true leaders of our country. With desire and determination, you can be one of them. At first, you might assume that it takes an extraordinary person to make such a break and define his or her own success, but the people in the following pages didn't think of themselves as extraordinary at the start of their journeys. The first step is to decide to be disobedient, to say to the forces of the status quo, "Nah, I'm going to do it differently." The second is to look around, to explore the possibilities—which is why we invite you to meet the people in this book.

As the stories reveal, breaking away can be scary at first and can come with a price. But it's usually well worth that price, and disobedience itself can be empowering and exhilarating. Moreover, breaking the corporate bonds is the twenty-first century's paramount struggle for the democratic soul of America. For the last twenty-five years, the power elites have been shutting out and knocking down the workaday majority of Americans who are "The Powers That *Ought to Be*," imperiously telling us, "You don't matter." Corporate interests have now seized control of our politics and government, work and leisure . . . our very lives and our sense of well-being.

If this is not worthy of rebellion, what is? Asserting your own values (fairness, justice, equal opportunity, stewardship, democracy) and placing human aspiration above corporate avarice is as important and as historic a struggle as were the fights for human dignity in the 1960s and 1970s and the labor struggles of the 1920s and 1930s to better the lives of working people and old folks. In the activist continuum of our country—a nation that was born in rebellion—it is our turn.

The people we highlight are not only enriching their lives, but creating a new, deeply democratic model for America, edging our country back onto the long road toward egalitarianism and the common good. Join them!

PART ONE

BUSINESS

"All serious daring starts from within."

—Eudora Welty

CHAPTER 1

Business without Greed

The telegram was the e-mail of its day. Sent by wire and hand-delivered in yellow envelopes by Western Union messengers, telegrams were yesteryear's "instant" communication. Many were clever, including one from movie star Cary Grant responding to a telegram sent by a reporter. The scribe wanted to know Grant's age, but since these wired messages were expensive and the company charged by the word, the reporter stripped his query to its essence:

HOW OLD CARY GRANT?

The reply was quick and equally terse:

OLD CARY GRANT FINE. HOW YOU?

Words matter. After all, they're the chief way we human types communicate ideas and meanings to one another. Unfortunately, just as words can be used to enlighten, they're also used by the devious and the self-serving to obfuscate, distort, and narrow. Insidiously, some of our country's broadest, most vibrant social concepts have been run through the establishment's word-wringer to squeeze out the richness and flatten the definition. Such big, juicy, vital, pulsating, essential ideas as "citizen," "consumer," and "community" have gotten the shrink treatment, and we'll get to all of them in subsequent chapters, showing how you can enlarge, elevate, and revitalize them.

But let's start with one concept that most Americans rarely consider: business.

What is business?

> *(Come on, you two, don't toy with us. What's to know about business? There's Wal-Mart, McDonald's, Exxon, AT&T, Safeway, Nike, and all those other brand names. Look at the logos on the tall buildings and sports arenas, or go to the mall, or just watch TV. Lookie here, I'm wearing a Mickey Mouse T-shirt and headed to Toys 'R' Us—now that's business, amigo.)*

Wrong. Those are merely examples of a particular and constricted form of business called the Corporation. Such branded behemoths don't represent the breadth and depth of business any more than piranhas represent the many wondrous species of fish. While multinational corporations are the most powerful and recognizable business structures today, they certainly are not the only way to organize commerce—and for both society and individuals, these massive syndicates turn out to be the least desirable way.

That's because a giant corporation exists solely for itself, operating strictly to enlarge its bottom line and enrich the wealthiest elites who own and run it. Corporations are artificial legal fictions (a scrap of paper, really) that let their owners reap profits without having to be personally responsible for any harm done in pursuit of those profits. The corporation itself has no feelings, no conscience, no heart, no soul, no morality, no shame—no butt to kick and no body to put in jail.

The humans who run these things operate within the confines of a rigid corporate ethos that has a military-like abhorrence of freewheeling ideas (as in, "When I want your opinion, soldier, I'll give it to you"). The closest one might come to institutional "spirit" can be found at Wal-Mart, where the morning shift is expected to come to work early for a group chant of the daily cheer. "Gimme a W!" shouts the shift manager. "W," barks the dutiful group. "Gimme an A!" And so on.

Big corporations are purposefully structured to be hierarchical, autocratic, regimented, secretive, antidemocratic, extractive, exploitative, avaricious, self-aggrandizing, absentee organizations that are out to grab as much profit as quickly as possible. Not that their mission is to do *intentional* harm (whether by downsizing workers, polluting our air and water, cheating consumers, crushing competitors, deceiving shareholders, corrupting government, stiffing communities, or generally running roughshod over society at large). But such harm is as inevitable as it is prevalent, due to the inherently selfish nature of these giants. If anyone or anything happens to be standing between top executives and an extra dime in profit, the "corporate ethic" commands that the executives bolt for the dime. Tough luck for whoever and whatever gets caught in the stampede.

This profit imperative is never debated where we peons might offer an opinion, but in the boardrooms, think tanks, and corporate conferences, it's the first consideration in all discussions. No less a light than Milton Friedman, the laissez-faire economic guru and patron saint of self-absorbed CEOs, once asked himself this question: "Do corporate executives, provided they stay within the law, have responsibilities in their business activities other than to make as much money for their stockholders as possible?"

I know you're dying of curiosity to know his answer, so here it is: "No, they do not."

Such a narrow ethic is a blank check for mischief on a grand scale. And mischief is what we're getting—there are so many corporate scandals that they no longer scandalize, so many greedheaded abuses that they're now the norm, with fresh ones in the news daily.

By the way, Friedman was being disingenuous when he tossed in the little prophylactic phrase that CEOs can do just about anything "provided they stay within the law." Come on, professor—you don't need a PhD to spell BS! Did he not know that we know that corporate executives and lobbyists buy the law, write the law, bend it, twist it, pervert it, slice-dice-grate-and-grind it finer than a Ronco Veg-O-Matic?

Most laws governing corporate behavior are weaker than Canadian hot sauce and rarely enforced. When the occasional watchdog agency does attempt enforcement, the punishment is usually nothing but a fine, which then gets reduced on appeal. It's cheaper to pay the fines than to stop the abuses. Companies can simply factor these assessments into their annual budgets as a normal cost of doing business, and (*warning: prepare for infuriating fact*) many of these civil fines for wrongdoing are merely deducted from the corporation's income tax!

Yeah, yeah, some of the Enron honchos got nailed in 2006 for looting the pocketbooks of thousands of shareholders, workers, and retirees. No surprise, since the top dogs, Ken Lay and Jeffrey Skilling, caused the jury to break into a collective fit of disbelieving guffaws when the two claimed innocence on the grounds that even though they were in charge, they had no clue—*no clue at all*—that there was hanky-panky going on. All they knew is that one day the corporation totally collapsed, and they found tens of millions of dollars in unexplained Enron cash in their own pockets. God works His wonders in mysterious ways.

(*Startling postscript*: After their convictions, Lay piously declared to the assembled media outside the courthouse, "We believe that God, in fact, is in control." I guess so! Only six weeks later, Lay was struck down by a sudden heart attack and died. Apparently God-Who-Is-In-Control called him home. Or . . . sent him elsewhere.)

Even more startling—at least to the hard-hit victims of Ken's finagling—is that after Lay croaked, a federal judge abruptly threw out the entire case against him! Citing a little-known and highly questionable judicial precedent called "abatement," the judge ruled that since the dearly departed could no longer pursue the appeals in his case, he must be deemed "innocent." So here's a guy who crashed his company and vaporized more than five thousand jobs and a billion dollars in employee pensions, a guy who walked away from the debacle with an ill-gotten $99 million in his pockets, a guy who was *found guilty* of six counts of fraud and conspiracy—and he gets his criminal conviction vacated, his trial record erased, and his indictment dismissed, as though nothing had ever happened.

Also, because Ken-the-dead-man is now officially innocent, the millions of dollars' worth of Enron cash that he stashed in his family estate stays there, rather than going toward restitution for the families he harmed. Even in death, the corporate honchos benefit from the law.

This bias is systemic, with corporate tentacles now tightly wrapped around our economy, government, environment, and culture. They're squeezing ever harder, strangling our society, choking the enormous grassroots potential of this great country. By defining business in the narrowest terms of global corporate interests, we sublimate all else to their bottom line, leaving only incidental room for the *multiple goals* of our community, including:

Time for family and friends

Personal satisfaction of workers

Encouragement of creativity

Promotion of discourse

Welcoming of dissent

Building of strong, local relationships

Good stewardship

. . . and, dare we add,

Fun

Laughter

The pursuit of happiness

A sense of shared purpose and belonging

A feeling of being respected and valued

The common good

Why should we give up all that? As individuals and as citizens of a country, why should we let a cabal of greedheads and boneheads define society's goals, reducing us to worker cogs and consumer ciphers in their lifeless machine?

(And away we go, Hightower, with another of your leftie, hate-America screeds, trying to rouse the rabble with all that pursuit of happiness crap. You know what your problems is, doncha, Jimbo? You're just antibusiness, that's what! Hey, that

old president, Calvin Coolidge, got it right years ago: "The chief business of the American people is business." Get over it.)

Me, antibusiness? Hardly. I grew up in business. My parents, "High" and Lillie Hightower, owned and ran a small wholesale magazine business, along with the Main Street Newsstand, in Denison, Texas. My first job was wrangling bundles of magazines into my daddy's delivery truck. (*Odd personal tidbit*: At twelve years old, I was entrusted with backing the truck down an alley and into position at the loading dock. Thus, I first learned to drive by going backward. Let the psychoanalysts make of that what they will.)

Antibusiness? I saw and deeply admired the entrepreneurial gumption and the hard, hard work my parents put into their business. I saw them respect and fairly reward the employees who worked with them. I saw how much they enjoyed their customers, always shooting the breeze and joshing with them, thereby making a visit to their store much more than a mere commercial transaction. I saw them under strain from time to time—they regularly had to wrestle with the bankers, needed to fight the chain stores, and ultimately had to survive a Wal-Mart. I saw them make a go of the business for some forty years, enabling them to provide a modest but happy middle-class upbringing for me and my brothers, Jerry and Larry.

Antibusiness? I worked my way through college as assistant manager of the chamber of commerce in Denton, Texas.

Antibusiness? As George W. might put it: "Not only am I in favor of business, *I are one!*" Since 1991, I've been the proprietor and "chief of stuff" at Saddle-Burr Productions, where I work with a small staff of smart, energetic people who handle the business of running my mouth—daily radio commentaries, weekly newspaper columns, monthly newsletter, frequent speeches, the occasional book, and so forth. I know both the joys and the tribulations of having to deliver a product in the marketplace, meet a payroll, cover the rent and the health care . . . and generally do business.

The essential question to ask is this: What kind of business? Today's corporations like to cite old Cal Coolidge's business-of-America line, but they conveniently leave out his follow-up thought, which came only three lines later: "Of course, the accumulation of wealth cannot be

"The idea of reinventing American capitalism sounds far-fetched, I know, and especially improbable considering the market-centered orthodoxy that reigns in conventional thinking. I can report, nevertheless, that many Americans are already at work on the idea in various scattered ways (though usually not with such sweeping declarations of intent). They are experimenting in localized settings—tinkering with the ways in which the system operates—and are convinced that alternatives are possible, not utopian schemes but self-interested and practical changes that can serve broader purposes. This approach seems quite remote from the current preoccupations of big politics and big business, but this is where the society's deepest reforms usually have originated in the American past. The future may begin among ordinary people, far distant from established power, who are brave enough to see themselves as pioneers."

—William Greider, *The Soul of Capitalism*

justified as the chief end of existence." Coolidge continued with "It's only natural that people seek some level of wealth, but there are many other things we want very much more." Then he garnished his point with this flower: "The chief ideal of the American people is idealism."

You don't hear that uplifting thought quoted very much, do you? Yet in terms of business alone, there are many ways to organize commerce—so unleash your idealism! Business can be designed around goals more worthwhile than merely funneling the mass of commercial wealth to a royal elite of CEOs and über-rich financial speculators. Among the structural possibilities are family enterprises, co-ops, partnerships, sole proprietorships, local markets, supply associations, bartering, buying clubs, and . . . (use your imagination).

The knee-jerk reaction is to dismiss alternatives out of hand as being small stuff, un-American, nonglobal, unworkable. But try telling that to the millions of Americans who're making smaller-scale, independent businesses work for them, their communities, and people around the world.

CHAPTER 2

Fair Trade

In Portland, Oregon, I recently saw a homemade bumper sticker declaring "Twit Happens." Between the two words was a photo of George W.'s face, with that quizzical look he so often gets.

Well, sometimes, "business happens," too—and it can turn out to be a good thing! In 1995, a new business happened, much to the amazement (and even bewilderment) of those involved.

That November, a terrific organization with the wonky name of Institute for Agriculture and Trade Policy (IATP) was concluding a weeklong discussion about agricultural trade with a small group of Mexican farmers and policy experts at IATP's Minneapolis office. Important stuff, but somewhat theoretical and mind-numbing. As the participants were packing up their papers and about to head out to medicate their glazed-over brains with several rounds of good Minnesota brewskies, Luis Hernandez suddenly interjected a jolt of ground-level reality to the week's erudite discussions: "You guys need to buy some of our coffee beans," he said to the IATPers.

Luis, you see, worked with an organic Mexican coffee growers cooperative, and while all this policy wonkishness had been nice, it had not sold a single coffee bean all week. Better policy will help the growers mañana, explained Hernandez, but to get to tomorrow, they need sales today.

"Uh, sure, sure," the weary IATP staffers assured Luis. "Now let's go drink some beer."

"No, I mean it," Hernandez insisted, and he proceeded to give an hour-long blackboard talk on how the beans move from impoverished Latino farmers through five middlemen to become a $3 Starbucks latte, with coffee farmers getting less than a penny out of that, which is why they need a way to bypass the scavenging middlemen. Instead of just *talking* about helping farmers, contended Hernandez, good-guy groups such as IATP should "get into" coffee, pay a decent price to the growers—and make good money themselves. "So," he said to his hosts, "how about it?"

"We don't have the money," pleaded the staff.

"No problem," said Luis. "We'll sell you the first container on credit."

"Yeah, well, okay, whatever," said the exhausted and dazed crew. "Now can we go drink beer?"

No more thought was given to this little exchange until December 5, when IATP headquarters received a startling phone call from a shipping company in Long Beach, California: "Where do you want your container of coffee beans shipped?" With thirty-eight thousand pounds of the green beans on its way, the IATP was yanked into the organic, fair trade coffee business.

The fair trade concept is simple: growers and their co-ops are dealt with directly, treated with respect, and paid a fair price that allows those on the land (farmers and workers) to live with dignity and practice environmentally sustainable agriculture. In the midnineties, the giant coffee purveyors that dominated the U.S. market (Philip Morris, Nestlé, Proctor & Gamble) scoffed at fair trade as fringy stuff, more social do-goodism and liberal meddling than real business. They bought their coffee beans through faceless transactions on the futures market, unconcerned that local speculators (known as "coyotes"—not a term of endearment) routinely ripped off the impoverished farmers, who were totally isolated from any knowledge about the world market. In 1994, a Nestlé executive sneered at the very notion of fair trade, happily declaring, "We have *no* relationship with coffee growers."

But in barely a decade's time, IATP and a hardy band of other coffee pioneers all across our country have brought the moral values of fair trade into the mainstream marketplace, with Starbucks, Green Mountain, Bruegger's—even McDonald's!—clambering onto the bandwagon.

When that first container arrived in Minneapolis, however, the IATP folks felt more like clumsy fools than moral business pioneers. Remember, these were policy people suddenly jettisoned into the roiling sea of commerce. Like a skit by Lucille Ball on the assembly line, things came at them at breakneck speed. First, they frantically scrambled to find a warehouse, but shortly after they stacked the pallets of coffee in it, the place went bankrupt, so they had to unstack, then restack them (by hand) in another site. Next they had to borrow money from friends and others just to hold the project together while they raced to locate green bean buyers, make sales, ship the goods, and collect payments.

But . . . it worked! They paid off the first container, then bought a partial container from a Guatemalan co-op, dedicating a portion of its sales to Guatemalan peace efforts, which led to the new business's name, Peace Coffee. In 1997, they shifted from selling green beans to roasting the beans, eventually getting what they proudly call "a big ol' roaster" and moving the entire operation out of IATP's basement into space about the size of half a basketball court.

Peace Coffee, with an energetic, enthusiastic staff of twelve, now has created trusted relationships with thirteen grower cooperatives in Colombia, Ethiopia, Guatemala, Mexico, Nicaragua, and Peru. While conventional coffee is trading on the commodities exchange for about a dollar a pound, and while the world price floor for fair trade coffee is $1.51 a pound, Peace Coffee pays its producers a minimum of $1.61 a pound.

Meanwhile, Peace Coffee also puts progressive values into its U.S. workplace, paying its employees about $16 an hour (roughly the median wage in Minnesota), plus health care and other benefits. Each

COFFEE COOPERATIVES

A big reason that Peace Coffee can do well while doing good is that it has embraced the same cooperative structures that the growers use. In 1999, it joined other fair trade roasters to found Cooperative Coffees, a sort of buying club for small, independent importers. Cooperative Coffees now has twenty-one members in the United States and Canada. Any one of these is too small to import a full container from a grower cooperative at one time, but by pooling their purchases, they and the farmers can deal in the volume that both need. Also, Cooperative Coffee can handle the paperwork and the importing details for the whole group, rather than each of the twenty-one roasters having to do its own separately.

The roaster co-op reinforces and amplifies the central message of its members: "We unite under the common desire to demonstrate through our example that alternative rules to trade policy are possible."

MEMBERS OF COFFEE COOPERATIVES

Each has its own distinct business model, array of coffees, and operating style. Visit them on the Web at www.coopcoffees .com/who, or stop by if you're in the neighborhood!

Roasters in the United States

Amavida Coffee, Santa Rosa Beach, FL

Fonseca Coffee, Philadelphia, PA

Bongo Java, Nashville, TN

Heine Brothers' Coffee, Louisville, KY

Café Campesino, Americus, GA

Just Coffee, Madison, WI

Cloudforest Initiatives, St. Paul, MN

Larry's Beans, Raleigh, NC

Coffee Exchange, Providence, RI

Los Armadillos, Austin, TX

Conscious Coffees, Breckenridge, CO

Peace Coffee, Minneapolis, MN

Dean's Beans, New Salem, MA

Pura Vida Coffee, Seattle, WA

Desert Sun, Durango, CO

Roasters in Canada

Alternative Grounds, Toronto, ON

Café Rico, Montreal, QC

Bean North, Whitehorse, YK

Equator Coffee, Almonte, ON

Café Cambio, Chicoutimi, QC

employee shares the job of delivering the product to coffee shops and other customers in the Twin Cities area. This is no small deal during the Northland's frigid winters (which, in my experience, last for approximately ten and a half months a year), because Peace Coffee has an ecologically friendly policy of year-round *bicycle delivery*! They hitch specially designed trailers to the bikes, pedaling some four hundred pounds of coffee within a forty-mile range of the roasting facility.

Your everyday corporate coffee executive would spew his morning sip of java right out of his nose at the very idea that a business should take such steps. Yet Peace Coffee defines fairness to growers, workers, and the environment as *integral* to its business success. They call it "a soulful cup."

Peace Coffee does all of this—plus making a financial success of the enterprise—while pricing its product in the midrange for upscale coffee ($8 to $10 a pound, retail). It sells about seventy-five hundred pounds of coffee every week, and not only is the company profitable, but it's also growing by 20 percent or so each year. "It's like riding a bucking bronco," said Scott Patterson, who was Peace Coffee's first staffer. "It's taken off, and I'm just trying to stay on."

CHAPTER 3

Cooperation Works

I magine a large, nationwide, profitable food business that espouses and proudly works toward these goals:

- *Market* the best-tasting, most nutritious and most wholesome foods possible.

- *Pay* a fair return to the farm families and the workers who produce the food.

- *Emphasize* production practices that result in ecological and economic sustainability.

- *Provide* a healthy human livelihood through quality employment, cooperation, organic values, and community growth.

- *Practice* environmental awareness in all aspects of business.

- *Promote* respect for diversity, dignity, and interdependence of human, animal, plant, soil, and global life.

Of course, no major corporation would hire any executive who even has the capacity to generate such goals, much less the chutzpah to suggest that they be made central to the company's business plan.

Fortune 500 CEOs have a vision that extends no farther than their own snouts, which is to say to tomorrow's stock price and their own platinum paychecks.

For the bigger vision, reflected in these far-reaching goals, you need a more expansive business structure. In this case, a cooperative.

In the mid-1980s, a handful of financially squeezed, politically frustrated Wisconsin farmers met around a kitchen table to face two hard realities: (1) the corporate middlemen were making all the money, not even paying producers enough to eke out a living; and (2) Congress and the White House were too cozy with the middlemen to take any action that would actually assist farmers. The market system was broken, the government was bought . . . and the farmers were going broke. Change would have to come from within.

Out of the farmers' conversation (the first of many that followed in other kitchens, barns, town halls, and such) came the creation in 1988 of a farmer-owned, democratically run cooperative that today includes some 950 farm families producing dozens of organic food products (milk, cheese, butter, eggs, meats, juices, etc.) in twenty-seven states, racking up $333 million in annual sales. The co-op bears the cumbersome name of Cooperative Regions of Organic Producer Pools, but you might recognize it more readily by its national brand name: Organic Valley.

THE UN-CORPORATION

"We were just a group of small farmers trying to launch something," said Jim Wedeberg, one of the co-op's seven original members. The "thing"—the structure itself—is important, for they were out from the get-go to build a business entity that wouldn't become a monster and devour them and their values. Jim said flatly, "We never even thought about organizing into a corporate structure." Attempting to squeeze their hopes and ideals into such a constraining form would've been as bad a fit as trying to put panty hose on a cow. To the contrary, they wanted to be the un-corporation.

Yet they were not starry-eyed about cooperatives, for they and other farmers have had less than joyous encounters with pseudo co-ops that long ago abandoned their democratic principles to become nothing but corporations in co-op costumes.

Still, a cooperative at least offered the possibility of real democratic control, so they chose this model, determined to get it right. As one of the farmers suggested, "Let's just write down what the big co-ops do, then let's do the opposite." Not a bad plan.

Naturally, they cared what the bottom-line results would be. Farming is a business, and they knew that Goal Number 1 was to band together so they could command a fair price for their products, make a little profit, and keep farming. But the bottom line definitely was not their only line. They cared just as deeply about protecting the land and the water where they lived, about being a community of supportive people, and about the welfare of the next generation of family farmers . . . and the next, and the next, and . . .

They sought to create a business entity in which their roles were not as mere shareholders (a term with a passive connotation, along

---

NAME THAT CO-OP!

For obvious reasons, the Cooperative Regions of Organic Producer Pools needed a brand name. Rather than commission a branding firm (yes, such things exist) to concoct a name, the co-op went to its roots. Everyone in the area got in on the name game—farmers, co-op employees, customers, neighbors, and even several cows were asked for ideas.

Ideas poured in, time dragged on . . . but nothing quite captured "it." Then, one bright morning, Jim Pierce, the co-op's milk hauler, was running his route up and down the scenic roads to pick up organic milk from the farms when he said to himself, What a beautiful valley this is! *Flash!* It came to him: Organic Valley. Simple, pure, beautiful. Back at the office, they cheered Jim, added the tagline "Family of Farms," and there it was, as organic as the product itself.

the lines of "Now you go sit on the porch and wait, while the executives take care of business"). Nor did the grander term of "owner" convey the fullness of what these farmers had in mind, for it's a possessive construct that doesn't encompass the richer social impact that they intended their business to have. So how to describe it? *Family.* Yeah, that was it. Organic Valley happily describes itself as "a big extended family," with its members working for one another, pulling together to enrich the whole as well as individuals. They launched a *business family*, in which everyone matters.

George Siemon is one of the farmers who was instrumental in the rise and internal strength of the co-op, serving as its chief executive since the co-op's beginnings in 1988. But George doesn't look, sound, or act much like your typical CEO—he even lists himself in the company's publications as the "C-E-I-E-I-O!"

Raised in a business family in Florida, he always wanted to work in nature, so he and his wife, Jane, moved to the rolling hills of Western Wisconsin, near the Upper Kickapoo River valley, to become organic farmers. They milked cows, worked with horses, grew most of their own food, and were embraced by the locals. The area's longtime farmers were generous with their knowledge and support. "I majored in old-timers," George said of his start-up, and he loved the people's wit, common sense, gumption, idealism, and commitment to community.

These human strengths are inherent in people throughout our country, from inner cities to suburbs to rural places. Unfortunately, in today's corporatized social ethic of "I got mine, you get yours," such qualities are rarely called forth for a common purpose.

In this case, they were as essential to Organic Valley's success as were the co-op's hard assets and no-nonsense business decisions. For example, take the board's decision at the very start to set a firm floor price on members' organic milk.

Here's what they did. Co-op milk haulers went around each day to collect the raw milk produced by each farm family. They then delivered and sold the whole load as a "pool" to wholesalers, processors, packagers, or even retailers. Pooling their milk gave the group more market clout than if each family went to market separately. By setting

MEET A FARMER

Travis Forgues grew up on a dairy farm in northern Vermont, right up against Lake Champlain and the Canadian border. He loved life on the farm but hated to see his parents constantly under stress just trying to make ends meet in a volatile milk market that was totally out of their control. In 1999 alone, 123 Vermont dairy farmers went under.

Seeing no future in farming, Travis's parents urged him to go to college and find other work. He studied computer science, married his high school sweetheart, and moved to "the city" (Burlington, population 40,000), but he kept yearning for the farm life. He convinced his parents to let him co-farm the family place with them, trying some new sustainable techniques.

That's when Jim Wedeberg showed up, pushing the Organic Valley concept. Not only did the Forgueses sign up, but Travis also recruited two neighboring farmers to join, thus assuring enough volume to justify the milk truck's making a regular run to their area.

Travis turned out to be quite a persuasive proponent of both organics and co-ops. After working the farm all day, he spent two to three hours each night trying to involve others. Today, twenty-two farm families (whose land had been destined to become housing developments) are part of the Organic Valley Family of Farms, living and working on more than six thousand acres, raising some fourteen hundred cows, producing six thousand gallons of organic milk a day, and earning nearly double what they made the old way. The Forgueses' farm itself, which could barely sustain one family under the conventional system, now supports two families with ease, including Travis and Amy's two young children.

a price floor, the co-op was saying to these buyers, "We'll not sell our premium product [organic milk] beneath this level, for we take great pride in its quality and value."

Of course, this approach works only if everyone sticks together. It's not easy. Prices fall, unprincipled buyers try to divide and break the co-op . . . stuff happens. In the lean times—and there were plenty of those in the early years as the co-op was trying to get its legs—there were very real financial and personal strains on the families, and it was tempting for any of the members to say, "Oh, hell, this isn't working. I'm gonna break away and take a dollar less on my organic milk."

But no one did. Although it was ten years before Organic Valley moved into the black, the co-op family held together and it even grew, increasing from the original seven to forty-eight farms. At one especially tough point in 1989 (board members had discovered that their fledgling business was in more debt than they thought), one member uttered an upbeat sentiment that instantly became the co-op's in-house mantra, helping them to get through whatever difficulties arise: "Anything worth having doesn't come easy."

The business strategy of setting a price floor was crucial to Organic Valley's success. But it was the members' idealism, gumption, commitment to community—and, especially, their ability to laugh in the face of hardship—that made the strategy work. They did something totally alien in the get-yours-now corporate world: they stuck with one another in order to build and make gains for everyone over the long haul.

Attitude matters. Soon after it started, the co-op decided to try processing some of its milk (rather than just selling the raw product). A couple of members went to a local company to have some cheese made, grated, and packaged. One of the company men was scornful of a bunch of farmers trying to become a sophisticated food business. "You guys are playing way out of your league," he said. To which one of the farmers said right back, "If you don't play out of your league, you don't ever get out of your league."

THE TURTLE

George Siemon wears a turtle pin. "There are all these flashy corporate CEOs out there," he told me. "They're the hares, racing full speed and getting all the attention. But Organic Valley is the turtle, moving steadily forward. And we're going to win the race, because our model of doing business is sustainable. Theirs is not.

"Corporate CEOs wake up in a sweat every morning," George said. "The first thing they do is check their stock price. Before they even brush their teeth! They live and die by Wall Street's valuation. So everything they do the rest of the day is about tomorrow's stock price.

"I don't even have to think about that. I can think full-time about serving farmers, the employees, the community—serving our mission. It's freeing. It's a better way to do business. A better way to live."

The turtle is definitely making progress, doing so well that it was comfortable in 2006 delivering a message to the biggest single marketer on the global block: Wal-Mart. The co-op's message was something this corporation never hears from suppliers: *No. Uh-uh. Bye-bye.*

This retailing colossus is now the world's largest seller of organic milk. Getting on Wal-Mart shelves is the ecstatic wet dream of practically every business executive involved in making any sort of product. From such mainstay giants as Proctor & Gamble to small start-ups, a company's presence in any or all of Wal-Mart's sixty-nine hundred stores is the very definition of corporate success—"Good God a'mighty, Bubba, we got it made now! Praise be to Sweet Jesus and Sam Walton, we're inside the Big Wally! Got our ticket punched and we're on the escalator straight up to corporate heaven! Someone give me an amen!"

The problem with being inside Wal-Mart is that it's a beast. It has no values beyond its own bottom line, and its affection for you and your product is based strictly on how cheaply you'll sell it. There's constant pressure on you to cut corners in your own business just to slice a fraction of a penny off the price you're charging this corporate behemoth. And forget long-term relationships—Wal-Mart buyers think loyalty is a river somewhere in the wilds of the Ozarks.

Still, when this beast decided to buff up its image by "going organic" a couple of years ago, it naturally reached out to Organic Valley. After a pretty heated internal debate, the co-op board chose

EARTH DINNER

Let's talk about what's in our dinner—and I don't mean trans fats, E. coli, red dye number 7, pig snouts, sex hormones, pesticides, and other uglies.

Instead, let's talk about history, music, art, farming, cooking, family memories, gardening, craftsmanship, regionalism, celebrations, taste, love, and all the other aspects of our culture that are embodied in every bite of our food. Too often, we eat meals without any thought of the myriad connections that any particular dish represents. To help reawaken those links in a way that can be both touching and fun, Organic Valley has come up with a novel idea for a social occasion: the Earth Dinner.

This involves simply throwing a dinner party organized around the remarkable role that food plays in our lives (besides keeping us alive, I mean). It can be a potluck dinner, an exquisite five-course meal, a simple buffet, a backyard picnic . . . whatever suits you. The key is to know something about the food—where it comes from, the history of some of the ingredients, or the cultural origin of the dishes. Invite friends and family of all ages and backgrounds—even add a farmer, if you know one! Then eat, talk . . . enjoy.

The goal is to get everyone thinking, reminiscing, telling stories, and laughing as the dinner progresses. Ask guests to share their very first food memory or to recall any family member who was a farmer, a gardener, a cheese maker, a cook, and so forth. Organic Valley's Earth Dinner Web site provides tips on everything from menus to party favors, as well as relating the experiences of people who've put together successful Earth Dinners. Also, a boxed set of forty-nine cards is offered, each one posing a question that keeps the conversation going.

Check them out at www.earthdinner.org.

to give it a try. Very quickly, though, Organic Valley's price was being undercut by Horizon, the brand name of the organic milk peddled by food giant Dean Foods Inc. Also, Big Wally was sucking up so much of the co-op's milk supply that it was having trouble meeting the needs of other retailers, from big outfits like Whole Foods to local health food stores.

Any first-year MBA student can tell you that the answer to this problem is rudimentary: increase your supply, pronto, and sell even cheaper than Horizon. Come on, buckaroo, squeeze more milk out of each cow, get more cows, rush more farmers into the co-op, merge with another milk company, do something, ANYTHING TO STAY ON THE SHELF!

No. Organic Valley wouldn't do it, because that's a short-term corporate strategy, not a sustainable approach. The co-op is not merely an organic producer, it's an *organic business* in which values are as important as volume. George said that the board and the members asked themselves these questions: "Who are our keepers? Which retailers have been with us in the past and will stick with us down the road?" Not Wal-Mart.

No one had ever pulled out of Wally, and the buyer was totally stunned. But, said George, "We're independent. We answer to ourselves, not to Wall Street, so we can do it. We can keep our soul."

A PARTNERSHIP SOCIETY

Even though Organic Valley is a business (a realm that normally celebrates and rewards self-serving greed), it is showing that a successful business can embrace the humanizing ethic of working for the common good. It has organized its business around what it calls the "partnership society," a collaboration among its farmers, employees, customers, and communities.

It's democratic in nature (and in action), with constant discussion and feedback from all involved. Siemon calls it the "dynamics of talking." There are regular conference calls and meetings, which—believe it or not—people are eager to join, because the topics have substance and people's opinions count. Since institutions eventually tend toward self-protecting bureaucracy, the co-op aggressively promotes a culture of openness and self-examination. George himself keeps a machete under his desk, brandishing it from time to time with shrieks of "Cut the bureaucracy!"

The Organic Valley partnership even succeeds at something that major corporations are abandoning: workplace fairness. Employees get decent pay, health care, retirement benefits, flextime, paid personal leave, advancement opportunities, training, low-cost lunches (organic, of course), and a comfortable place to work (shoes optional in the warm months!).

Also, real profit sharing. There have been years of no profit, but when it does show its happy face, the money is allocated on a model that recognizes the contributions that all make to the business success:

- 45 percent goes to the farmers.
- 45 percent goes to the employees.
- 10 percent goes to the communities.

This is no small deal. In 2006, a good year for the co-op, the employees' share averaged $3,000 each, which goes into their retirement fund.

Siemon said, "We're a social experiment masquerading as a business." Twenty years into it, the experiment is a proven success, offering a real-life model for business . . . and for our larger society.

Oh, one more important point. Organic Valley holds an annual summer festival for its members—they put up an enormous tent on a beautiful hillside outside of LaFarge, serve the members' own organic foods, provide great local music, and pour a waterfall of fine Wisconsin beer. DeMarco and I have attended, wallowing in the pure joy of this event, so we can attest that this co-op knows how to throw a party!

CHAPTER 4

Socially Responsible

William Henry Vanderbilt, a nineteenth-century railroad czar and robber baron (who, at the time, was the self-proclaimed richest man in the world), had his own clear vision of the natural order of business: "The railroads are not run for the benefit of the dear public. That cry is all nonsense. They are built for men who invest their money and expect to get a fair percentage of the same." In 1882, Ol' Vandy snorted out a dictum that pretty well expresses how top corporate executives through the years have viewed the notion that business has any social responsibility: "The public be damned!"

But, lo and behold, at the dawn of our twenty-first century, there has arisen a contrarian ethic of entrepreneurship that says business has more than a responsibility; it has a moral obligation to be a force for creating a better world. This is not about Microsoft doling out charitable donations or ExxonMobil sponsoring an Earth Day litter-cleanup project, but about a growing number of creative enterprises that focus on the public good as part and parcel of their business mission.

The products or services of these businesses are focused squarely on some of society's most difficult issues (poverty, illness, pollution, lack of affordable housing, etc.). Rather than viewing them as intractable problems, innovative entrepreneurs are looking at these unmet needs in business terms and addressing them for what they are: underserved markets. Indeed, they are *mass* markets with a huge, pent-up demand, yet today's barons of capitalism have not had the savvy or the ingenuity to enter them. Of course, these are not markets that promise the platinum level of profits that today's "men who invest" require.

BANKING ON THE POOR

To find an alternative business ethic to "the public be damned," look no further than the man who received 2006's Nobel Peace Prize, Muhammad Yunus. An economics professor in Bangladesh, he became a banker to the poor, reaching out to a truly massive market made up of millions of Bangladeshis whom traditional bankers could not imagine being worthy customers: abandoned wives, destitute widows, rickshaw drivers, landless laborers, and beggars.

Yunus's first venture into the world of banking was in 1972. He was teaching what he smilingly called "elegant theories of economics" when he came upon a group of forty-two villagers near his university. They wanted only the smallest amount of capital to put into a real-life economic venture. He "loaned" them $27 out of his own pocket, not expecting to see it again. However, the villagers put the money to work right away, and soon returned to pay Yunus back in full. Wow, he thought, if you can make so many people happy with such a small amount of money, why shouldn't you do more of it?

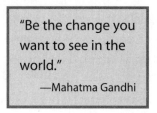

"Be the change you want to see in the world."

—Mahatma Gandhi

So, enlisting others, he set up Grameen Bank (in the Bangla language, "Bank of the Villages"), determined to see what the power of banking could do if harnessed to the huge social goal of economic development among the poor. He reasoned that if small amounts of capital are placed into the hands of the poor, "these millions of small people with their millions of small pursuits can add up to create the biggest development wonder."

Grameen made tiny micro-loans (an average of $130, and many as low as $12) to impoverished rural people who'd been considered "unbankable." Throwing all rules out the window, Grameen required zero collateral for the loans and did not require anyone to sign a single piece of paper. Yunus said that the lender-borrower relationship was "based on mutual trust, accountability, participation, and creativity."

It worked. Borrowers invested their meager loans in such assets as a milk cow, a supply of bamboo, or spools of yarn, turning these into cheese, handmade stools, clothing, and other money-making products. Whole villages lifted themselves up, both financially and in spirit. The system became self-sustaining because, as Yunus flatly said, "The poor always pay back."

As documented in numerous independent studies, these micro-loans have helped to raise incomes, empower women, and improve educational levels throughout Bangladesh. Today, Grameen Bank has 7 million borrowers, 97 percent of whom are women. It has 2,300 branches serving 7,500 villages, covering 90 percent of all the country's villages.

With Grameen having proved the concept, micro-lending is now becoming established elsewhere around the world, including in our own U.S. of A. High-finance megadeals still capture all of the news, but they're no longer the only way to go. In banking, small can be big.

AFFORDABLE AND PROFITABLE

In any city across our land, you can hear the power saws screaming and nail guns *ka-pow*ing as developers put up house after house. In certain neighborhoods, that is.

The luxury market—$500,000 homes to $5 million McMansions (and up)—is well-served. But try to find something affordable for the great majority of folks. I'm not talking only about low-income families, but also those earning $35,000 to $50,000 a year, such as schoolteachers or firefighters who're unable to get a house or even an apartment they can afford in the cities they serve.

"Can't be helped," snap the developers. "No way could we build places in town for people like that. That's why God created suburbs and commuter highways."

Martin Dunn proved that they're full of horsestuff. In the complex and expensive real estate market of New York City, this forty-year-old builder has been putting up apartment complexes for those on the lower rungs of the economic ladder. Dunn and team focus their rental projects on working families making less than $50,000 a year. "I used to think 'developer' was a four letter word," said Dunn, who spent his early years with nonprofits that fought landlords and quick-buck developers. "But I wanted to do new things, and I found a place for entrepreneurship based on social values, taking financial risks to do the right thing."

Look at Palmer's Dock in Brooklyn, New York, a 113-unit apartment building that his company, Dunn Development, will complete in the winter of 2007. It's in the rapidly gentrifying Williamsburg neighborhood, where working-class people who grew up there are being pushed out by high-dollar developments. Palmer's Dock, however, will make apartments affordable for a range of modest-income families, for it will have a five-tier price structure, with rents running from $398 to $920 a month. "There's not just one income level for working-class people," Dunn pointed out, and this project will bring together those making from about $17,000 a year on up to those making a little less than $50,000.

That's serving an enormous need right there, but in most of his projects, Dunn also mixes in studio units for people with psychiatric disabilities (many of them homeless, including veterans returning from Iraq), developmental disabilities, or HIV/AIDS. Called "supportive housing," these complexes include on-site social services and counseling. The idea is to get people with special needs into a neighborly environment where they can be accepted and thrive.

These are not mere buildings but are truly creative expressions of the developer craft—economically, artistically, and socially. They are hardly the stereotypically sterile, sometimes shoddy construction that lower-income housing often is. Instead, Dunn strives to create "the nicest building on the block." He uses the latest in green technology (Palmer's Dock, for example, includes a three-thousand-square-foot green roof and a landscaped rooftop terrace, and it is so energy efficient that most residents will see their utility bills go down by a third). The buildings have beautiful architectural details, bright interiors, landscaped gardens, play areas, large community rooms with kitchens for social events, library-computer rooms, and other amenities. Low income doesn't have to mean substandard.

Financing comes from a combination of private and public sources, ranging from commercial banks to tax credits for low-income housing. Dunn's company has now developed eleven of these complexes in Brooklyn and the Bronx, typically earning 8 to 10 percent of the cost of the buildings as its share. "We are for-profit, but we are mission driven," he said. "We are not looking to do the real estate that makes the most money. We want to do something important that still provides us a reasonable return."

HEALTHY HEALTH CARE

Who would've thought that in the moral morass of what is now called the health "industry," the flower of social responsibility could still bloom?

The *industry* is controlled by insurance middlemen, HMO chains, and rip-off drug makers—all putting profits over patients. The *industry's* lobbyists impose public policies that leave forty-seven million of our fellow Americans with no health plan whatsoever, while tens of millions more hold miserly plans that provide very little balm in times of need. The *industry* has created such a screwed-up system that we Americans spend more each year on health care ($6,280 per capita) than people in any other country, yet the treatment we get ranks a pathetic thirty-seventh in the world.

But there's good news: rising from the grassroots in every area of the country, health professionals and businesses are bringing an enterprising spirit to this dysfunctional system, reaching communities of people who've been shut out, and showing the way to put the "care" back into health care.

Charlie Alfero is one of these people. Working with both private and public health institutions in New Mexico for nearly thirty years, he is some combination of agitator and administrator,

---

"CONCIERGE CARE"

To exacerbate the gross inequality that already characterizes the U.S. health-care system, some doctors in recent years have been jettisoning the bulk of their patients and opening boutique practices that cater exclusively to the well-heeled. In exchange for annual cash retainers that can reach $10,000 per person, these doctors-to-the-elite provide such touches as fruit salad and sponge cake in their waiting rooms. Not that patients need to wait—their money buys twenty-four-hour cell phone access to the doctor, same-day appointments, house calls . . . and the doc will even go with them to see specialists!

The doctors can dramatically increase their incomes while drastically cutting the number of patients they see. Where do the rejected patients go? Away.

---

adept at figuring out how to get quality care delivered to rural out-posts that the corporatized medical system has largely abandoned. Moreover, he sees health care as key to reviving the *economic* health of those areas.

Charlie's outpost is Hidalgo County. Where? Look at the bottom left corner of a map of the "Land of Enchantment" and you'll see a boot heel. That's Hidalgo, a remote but picturesque stretch of the Old West that was once crossed by the Butterfield Stagecoach line, then the Southern Pacific railroad, and now I-10. The boot heel is a long way from any city—Tucson is 150 miles west, El Paso 150 miles east, and Albuquerque 300 miles north.

It has been a hard-hit area. Copper companies used the place up before pulling out in the 1970s and 1980s, leaving Hidalgo mostly a ranching economy. Some six thousand people live there, with a lot of poverty among them. The local hospital closed in 1979. The last doctor left in 1983, and the county was unable to entice another one to move in. There was an obvious need and demand for health services, but Hidalgo is hardly the sort of lucrative market that such profit-hungry chains as Hospital Corporation of America are willing to consider.

The county's leaders realized they would have to put something together for themselves. So in 1994, they asked the state rural health office to send some experts to Lordsburg, the county seat, to help guide them. One who came was Charlie Alfero. Years previously, he had attended a small college up the road in a neighboring county, and he was glad for the chance to revisit a region he loved.

Alfero had been working with the rural outreach program of the state university's medical school, and he remembered from his earlier time in the boot heel that despite economic difficulties, the people of the area shared strong egalitarian values. He felt that they might do big things. He arrived with a vision: the people there could create a health commons of their own design—a community complex that would provide one-stop service for medical, dental, and mental health care, with family support services and economic development built in.

Most of Hidalgo's residents have lived in the county all of their lives and have an attachment to the area and to one another. "We stick together; we help each other in times of need," said Irene Galven, now the city clerk. It was this sense of community, the residents' willingness to throw in on projects to benefit everyone, that inspired Alfero to throw in with them.

It was not a simple project. For nearly four years, Charlie made the six-hundred-mile round-trip commute each week from his home in Albuquerque to Lordsburg to work with eager locals to establish Hidalgo Medical Services (HMS), get it on its feet financially, and get it moving—one small step at a time.

- On July 1, 1995, HMS opened its doors in one wing of the old hospital, offering health services two days a week. Four doctors from Silver City (fifty-five miles from Lordsburg) rotated to the clinic, each doing one day every two weeks.

- In the fall of 1996, HMS was able to add a full-time nurse practitioner, meaning that Hidalgo County had daily medical service for the first time in thirteen years.

- In the spring of 1997, HMS's proposal for rural outreach was funded by two small but crucial federal programs, the Community Health Center and the Office of Rural Health Policy, thus allowing the clinic to expand its services and hire a full-time family physician.

- In 1998, for the first time in county history, dentistry was made available on a part-time basis. Also, with the clinic becoming a viable enterprise (it now occupied about 60 percent of the old hospital), Charlie Alfero left Albuquerque to become the CEO of HMS.

From the start, Charlie understood that the key to success would be building broad support—enthusiasm, even—throughout the county and gaining the trust of all involved. In addition to board members who could bring a bit of clout to the cause (hometown bankers, lawyers, local officials, and certain retired professionals), he enlisted some of the clinic's patients to serve (today, 100 percent of the board members are patients). He preached the democratic ethic that the larger community had to be invested in HMS, literally making it theirs and recognizing that "each person's success helps strengthen the whole."

Alfero took public involvement a step further by bringing ordinary residents inside to serve as a direct, integral, and very effective part

---

A PAIN IN THE TOOTH

When dental service was brought to Hidalgo County in 1998, it was the dentist who needed the Novacaine, for it was a long haul. Once a month, he flew in on the early a.m. flight from Albuquerque, landing at the Greater Intercontinental Municipal Airport in Silver City. There he climbed into a pickup truck that HMS kept there for him, took the dirt road for twenty-five miles to the highway, then drove on to the Lordsburg clinic, where an improvised dental office was rigged up. He spent three days seeing patients and slept at nights in a single-wide trailer the clinic kept nearby. After he saw his last patient on the third day, he drove back to Silver City, parked the pickup, and caught the last flight back to Albuquerque. Dentistry on the fly!

of the health delivery system itself. They were enlisted to be *promatoras de salud* (promoters of health). These community outreach workers, trained in the management of such chronic diseases as diabetes (a huge problem in this region), literally spread the reach of HMS, traveling out to smaller settlements and isolated ranches and bringing medical help, information, news, connection, and . . . well, care. "I think I've always been a *promatora*," declared Elva Quimby, a fiftyish former cosmetologist. "I just thrive on helping people."

Step-by-step, service was expanded, gaining the attention and the support of health professionals and funders outside of the boot heel. A little more capital was raised, another nurse or physician arrived, and before long HMS had become not only a strong medical center, but also the largest economic engine in the county. Alfero contended that if the strongest local asset is a health clinic, go with it! Why try to get some out-of-state conglomerate to reopen the copper smelter when you've got a clean, community-supported enterprise creating jobs, generating small business growth, and making people healthier?

A dozen years after opening its doors, HMS has become the health commons it was envisioned to be. On its tenth anniversary, it opened the doors of its new twenty-two-thousand-square-foot clinic in Lordsburg, a modern, full-service facility with nine exam rooms, lab and X-ray rooms, a dental clinic with six chairs, and offices to deal with mental health problems, substance abuse, and family support needs. It has a staff numbering more than 140, operating on a budget of more than $10 million a year.

In addition to Lordsburg, HMS now has clinics in six other communities in two counties, including one in Silver City, where it originally had to go to find doctors who were willing to come to Hidalgo twice a week.

"I didn't deliver health care," Alfero noted. "I'm not even a doctor. I just gave people an idea, pointed them in a direction, and they built this themselves. People who rely on external forces to determine their future are going to find a bad future. The people in this area are showing what health care can be if we invest in people, not in the layers of intermediaries looking to make money off a top-heavy system. Our country needs more clinics like this."

EDUCATING TOMORROW'S EXECUTIVES

MBA programs have long been considered the Black Hole of Ethics, the place where future CEOs go to get their graduate degrees in greed and learn to set aside all those pesky kindergarten lessons about playing fair, telling the truth, sharing your cookies, cleaning up your own messes, and so on. (*Note*: For a case study on the effectiveness of these programs, look to George W. Bush, Harvard MBA, 1975.) Scores of business schools hand out about a hundred thousand of these Master of Business Administration degrees every year, and what students are taught (or not taught) helps to determine the corporate culture.

"Ethics stays in the preface of the average business science book."

—Peter Drucker, maverick business guru

Hark! What's that noise I hear? Why, it's the rumblings of a rebellion rising from the most unlikely of sources: MBA students. They're saying that they want more from their professors than the rote corporate orthodoxy of "Maximize shareholder value" and "How to make a deal." They want to see the words "social responsibility" and "ethics" placed in the center of the MBA curriculum.

Appalled by the ongoing corporate scandals, stock-option cheating, environmental abuse, tax dodging, and the general Enronization of the corporate culture, a new generation of business students is out to bridge the disconnect between corporate profit and the social deficit. Most significantly, this movement is not interested in more corporate "philanthropy" or image-buffing. The students are going to the heart of the problem, arguing that "profitability" must include social and environmental results, as well as financial. They are insisting that business schools and their graduates must broaden the definition of business success beyond the singular notion of wealth accumulation for its own sake.

A 2006 online survey of twenty-one hundred students in eighty-seven MBA programs produced encouraging results:

- 81 percent believe that corporate executives should "work toward the betterment of society." (Yes, that's a vague goal, but note that only 18 percent believed that most corporations now do this.)

- 89 percent said executives should take social and environmental impact into account when making business decisions.

- 78 percent said the subject of corporate social responsibility should be integrated into the MBA core curriculum.

B-schools do much of their teaching by the case-study method, showing students models of real-life "successes" whom they should emulate. The studies tend to feature such corporate demigods as Jack Welch, the former honcho of GE, who is famous for ruthlessly (even gleefully) whacking workers while lining his own pockets with tens of millions of dollars in compensation.

Today's students, however, are seeking out their own models of success that they find more worthy of emulation. One company that they point to is Patagonia, founded in the 1970s by outdoor enthusiasts

"Someday hence . . . Americans will be talking again about the fundamentals, asking themselves if it is possible to alter the system in various ways and how they might proceed. We will be arguing anew, for instance, over the terms and conditions of work, and about the ways in which investment and production are organized. We may ask ourselves why the decision making in important institutions of business and finance is so closely held among a relative few when their decisions have such great impact on our lives at work and at home. We may explore more rigorously how our savings are deployed as investment capital and whether the results are pleasing or alarming. Indeed, why does the economic system seem so indifferent, even hostile, to the intangibles in life that have the deepest meaning for people and society? We might even ask ourselves: What *is* the meaning of wealth now that America is so awesomely wealthy?"

—William Greider, *The Soul of Capitalism*

Yvon and Malinda Chouinard to market environmentally sustainable outdoor clothing and gear. Even its mission statement differentiates this company from the usual self-serving corporation: "Make the best product, cause no unnecessary harm, and use business to inspire and implement solutions to the environmental crisis."

It has been a pioneer in doing just that. Patagonia was the first outdoor apparel firm to use recycled soda bottles as fleece, the first to make mass-market use of organic cotton, and the first to commit to "green buildings" in all of its operations.

Patagonia goes even further by imposing an "earth tax" on itself, donating 1 percent of sales to grassroots environmental groups. It gives its one thousand worldwide employees paid leave to take up to two months a year as Patagonia Interns working for the environmental group of their choice.

It also prides itself on retaining employees by paying well, providing good benefits, promoting from within, offering flexible schedules, and having on-site day care. It does this while enjoying 2006 sales of $276 million and making a healthy profit each year.

Patagonia's success is based on what the company calls a Virtuous Cycle:

Commit to strong social and environmental results,

↓

Attract local customers and dedicated employees, which

↓

Improves sales, productivity, and financial performance of the company, which

↓

Facilitates further commitment to social and environmental results.

This is the sort of business that a growing number of MBA students want to learn more about, and they're pressuring their schools to teach this broader concept of success. A sign of these new times is the rise of Net Impact. This network of MBA students and grads has more than ten thousand members and 130 chapters (including chapters in twenty-nine of the top thirty MBA schools, as ranked by *Business Week*). Its mission is to build a network of new leaders who are committed to using the power of business not just for the benefit of a few wealthy shareholders and CEOs, but for the greater good.

Obviously, there's a very long way to go, but MBA programs at such schools as Duke, Harvard, Loyola Marymount, Michigan, and North Carolina are responding by moving social and environmental issues to the mainstream of their teaching. As one student bluntly assessed the need: "It all comes down to the fact that business is seen as one thing, social responsibility as something on the side. We need to see a link between business and social responsibility."

CHAPTER 5

Putting Workers in Charge

Whether their jobs are in an office, a factory, a shop, or wherever, when workers get together on break or for a couple of beers after work, chances are that there is much discussion, laughter, and rolling of eyes about the latest idiocy committed by their bumbling bosses. This is why "Boss Day" (yes, it actually exists—mark your calendar for October 16!) is not celebrated as a major holiday anywhere in our country.

A common refrain coming out of these sessions is: "Man, if only they'd turn this place over to us, we could really get something done."

Increasingly, this comment is more than idle chitchat. It's the spark of a growing economic movement for more workplace democracy. Rather than just gripe about the bosses and laugh at them, workers are *becoming* the bosses. They're forming worker cooperatives: businesses owned and democratically governed by the paid workers.

While this gets practically zero coverage by the national media, more than 250 of those unique economic flowers are striving to push their way upward in cities across America. The co-ops come in all lines of business, including food processors, high-tech firms, grocery stores, photovoltaic manufacturers, publishers, restaurants, engineers, construction firms, computer consultants, and financial institutions. While none of these are big companies by Wall Street standards, all are substantial, both financially and as models for structuring business ownership, management, and goals differently—that is, more democratically.

For most of them, whether their roots go back to the creative experimentation of the 1960s or they have taken root more recently, it has been no easy chore to establish themselves. Getting a worker co-op going (much less keeping it going) can be as frustrating as trying to organize a cat parade. Banks don't like the small and unconventional; venture capitalists are searching for a 50 percent return; our culture teaches that workers are to work and bosses are to boss; the education system rarely offers courses or degrees in cooperative principles and worker management; corporate newspapers and broadcasters are dismissive of workplace democracy; and workers themselves can get tripped up by egos and infighting.

A friend in politics once told me, "Not only are the odds against you, so are some of the evens!" Yet many have made it, some are thriving . . . and more are giving it a try. These are important enterprises that can be enormously satisfying and financially rewarding for all involved. That's why so many savvy and scrappy Americans are defying the odds (and challenging the evens) to build this grassroots business movement.

CALL ME A CAB

We all know the punch line to the old "Call me a cab" joke: "Okay, you're a cab." But in 1979, a determined group of cabbies in Madison, Wisconsin, decided to call themselves a cab *company*. And now they are one.

I first encountered Union Cab Cooperative early one morning in 2000 when I asked a Madison hotel clerk to call a taxi for me. On the ride to the airport, I struck up a conversation with the driver, who proudly informed me that I was riding in the car of a worker-owned company. He said he was one of the founders of the co-op and that they'd come a long way, enduring lots of struggles. "But it's been worth the ride," he told me, for he'd been able to raise a family, send his kid to college, and live a modest, middle-class life. All of this as a cabdriver—not a job known for decent pay, long-term employment, or generating much worker enthusiasm.

But let's roll back to the mid-1970s, when a group of drivers in Wisconsin's capital city got fed up with the situation at Checker Cab, where they were being paid only 40¢ an hour, with no benefits and no rights. They were sent out in unsafe cars (axles broke, a wheel came off one while the car was moving, some had no heat in the dead of Wisconsin's brutal winter, etc.), there was no process for promotion, and drivers were generally treated with all the respect of a Kleenex. The drivers were mostly young—some were coming out of college, others were Vietnam vets, many were from blue-collar families—and they all had the "ain't-gonna-take-it-no-more" attitude of the times.

In July 1976 (coincidentally, the bicentennial of the Declaration of Independence), they took their first rebellious step by trying to unionize. Dave Everitt (still with the co-op) approached the Retail Clerks union, an organizing committee was formed, 75 percent of Checker workers signed certification cards, and a general meeting

---

A LESSON FROM LES

Not long ago, I took a cab in Austin, Texas, and Les was my cabbie. He told me that he'd just been driving a couple of well-heeled banker types when he passed a car with a bumper sticker demanding "A Living Wage for All!" One of the gents said to the other in a sort of smirking tone, "What the hell does that mean?"

Les couldn't help himself. He said he violated cabbie Rule Number 1 by taking his eyes from the road and turning to face his backseat fares: "It means when you go out to work in the morning, you come home with more money than you left with." Les said it was a pretty quiet ride the rest of the way.

was called for the union representatives to meet their potential new members.

It was a disaster. When the union reps arrived, they found a roomful of cabbies deep into several cases of beer, with sweet-smelling herbal smoke billowing out the doors. Shortly afterward, the union said, "No, thanks," leaving the drivers feeling betrayed and fearful of losing their jobs.

But they held firm, reached out to other unions, and in the fall signed an agreement to join the Laundry and Dry Cleaners International Union (LDIU).

The what?! Well, yes, it might seem like an odd fit, but one of the cabbies knew Tom Kiesgen, the organizer of LDIU, and Kiesgen took a sincere interest in representing the group. "I found them to have a great deal of potential," Kiesgen said. "There was a lot of energy there. Here were people with ability, intelligence, and good hearts who were willing to help each other out. They were left hanging, and we moved on it."

Taxi companies, however, are hardly union friendly, and the boss at Checker welcomed his new LDIU colleagues by trumping up reasons to dump anyone who'd been on the organizing committee. Then, to test the resolve of the workers, Checker stalled contract negotiations for months. The cabbies showed the owner more resolve than he could stand by going on strike in September 1977, with 99 percent of the employees walking off the job. Four days later, Checker signed.

With this success, the members really bonded, which is not easy for taxi drivers since they're mostly alone in their cabs and vying against one another to get the best fares. "Now suddenly we were working as a unit," said one of the drivers.

Unfortunately, the owner stayed nasty. He refused to deal with grievances, tried to split workers from the union, and, in September 1978, walked away from negotiations on a new contract. This led to a second strike that brought three months of confrontations and anxieties. But it also generated a growing camaraderie among the members, and they came up with some clever labor actions (for example, when the owner tried to bring in scab drivers to make airport runs, the union chartered a bus, drove to the airport, and offered free rides into the city as an alternative to taking a scab cab). Again, nearly 100 percent of workers supported the strike, as did the Madison community. The union was winning.

Then, just in time for Christmas joy, news came that the owner was bailing out and shutting down Checker Cab, leaving the cabbies with a union, but no jobs.

Luck and Pluck

"Well, why not us?" That was the attitude of many of the discarded Checker drivers—"Why not start our own cab company?" After all, who had done the driving, dispatching, maintenance, bookkeeping, and all the other chores involved in running the company? Not the boss—them! They figured that among their ranks, they had enough expertise to be successful in the taxi business. Later, one admitted, "Our desire to form a cab company was greater than our realization of how difficult it would be."

In January 1979, five of the cabbies decided to form a worker-owned company, stepping off the cliff and fashioning their wings as they went. The five founders split up the tasks of finding a lawyer, applying for taxi permits from the city, getting an FCC radio license, making financial projections, and so on. The one who was best at numbers drew up a business plan, calculating that they needed $150,000 to start up. But who was going to front a bunch of unemployed cab drivers with that kind of change?

At first, no one. This was a dicey time. While scrambling for capital, they decided to organize not merely as a worker-owned company, but also as a cooperative, for this both reflected their values and opened up brighter funding prospects.

The five, plus a couple of others, raised money from friends and family members; after a community appeal, the people of Madison put up a few thousand dollars in donations of $25 each; and a city-sponsored development fund came through with a loan, which loosened up other loans from the Small Business Administration and a local bank, giving them the lift they needed. On October 29, 1979 (after a hectic week of car buying and office construction), Union Cab

Cooperative opened for business with eleven used cars and an average wage of 80¢ an hour.

Then trouble started for real. Union Cab did not yet have a listing in the Yellow Pages, gasoline prices were spiking, and the co-op lost $35,000 in the first three months. The bankers got fidgety—never a pretty sight.

But from out of the darkness, Lady Luck suddenly smiled, casting three rays of hope upon the endangered co-op. The first came in February 1980 when the Madison city council, recognizing the unexpected financial squeeze caused by fuel prices, allowed the city's two taxi companies to boost their rates. Ten weeks after that, the second ray of luck shone down when the other taxi company closed, a victim of a community backlash against its truly horrific service and Union Cab's fresh, friendly alternative.

One week later, the brightest beam radiated from above: Madison's bus drivers went on strike. Grabbing the opportunity, the co-op quickly added five more cabs and turned the bus strike into a three-month bonanza for cabbies, giving the company the financial strength it needed to keep moving forward.

Sometimes the good news is also the bad news. In the early eighties, Union Cab was doing well. It moved into expanded facilities, added new services (such as parcel deliveries and airport limousines), and brought in new members of the co-op. With rapid growth, however, came dissension. "Size dictates some changes," said former general manager Steve Krumrei. "When you have over a hundred people, you can't have the same intimacy as you can when you've got a group of twenty or thirty people."

In 1984, the founding cohesiveness was waning, and internal conflicts flared. Four seats on the board of directors were open that year, but they drew only four candidates. Morale was falling, and some openly questioned whether the co-op had lost its "heart, soul, and spirit."

In such times, a family needs to reach out for help, and Union Cab did. From its start, the co-op had benefited from the advice and support of other cooperatives in the area (such as the great co-op radio station WORT, and the board turned to it again). Union Cab also received assistance from a national group called the Inter-Community Cooperative Council to reorganize its management structure. By 1985, the four available seats on the board drew eleven candidates, demonstrating that members were taking a renewed interest in directing their co-op and its enterprise. As one member said about this period of organizational evolution, "We were like a teenager trying to become an adult."

Opportunities

John McNamara had graduated from the state university in Madison in 1988. He was working as a bartender and pondering graduate school when he became intrigued by the co-op. He signed on as a driver that summer, thinking it would be just a rest stop on the road of life. He's still with Union Cab. After serving on the board for eight years, John moved from behind the wheel into the office to learn the business side and now serves as accounts manager. In addition, he has finally gotten around to graduate school, recently enrolling to study part-time for a master's degree in cooperative management.

CARING FOR CABBIES

In 1992, the co-op was interested in making a health plan available to members. John McNamara and others attended a conference of taxi companies and asked owners there what they were doing to provide health coverage for their employees. They were met by a sort of stunned silence. Then one asked, "Why would you want to?"

They persisted in their search and found a health and dental plan for the members, with the cooperative paying 55 percent of the premium. They are not satisfied (it costs a lot and doesn't do enough) so they are working to improve the plan. But still, Union Cab is one of the few cab companies in the country that offers health coverage to its workers.

Why did he stay? "Because I was interested in different ways of doing things, and people are given opportunities here. You're not just a cog in some machine. You can participate in a way that matters."

Today, Union Cab Cooperative is the largest of three taxi companies in Madison and the third largest in the state. It still has ups and downs (as any business does), but the co-op is now firmly rooted in the community, bearing fruit for all involved:

- Annual revenues of $6 million.

- More than two hundred employees, most of them whom drive at least one shift (every employee—from general manager to janitor—is a voting member of the co-op).

- An average wage of $14.18 an hour (roughly $28,000 a year), well above Madison's living wage standard of about $11.00 an hour.

- Sixty-three taxi vehicles, including wheelchair-accessible mini-vans and airport limos.

- Three full-time mechanics and two part-time, doing all the maintenance work for the co-op.

- A full-service taxi facility (now owned by the co-op), including a three-bay maintenance shop, an on-site fueling station, and a large office with a six-person dispatch center, a lunchroom, and a drivers' room.

- A steady growth pattern, with Madison's population increasing and customer satisfaction with Union Cab running at 90 percent, tops in the city.

Equally important is the ability of Union Cab to retain its cooperative spirit. Its slogan is "Democracy in Motion"—and, yes, of course, T-shirts are available! The co-op works hard to make this more than a slogan: board and other elections continue to draw healthy participation; there are seventy-nine separate positions for member involvement, and each one consistently draws at least two members seeking to serve; the general manager must come from within the co-op's membership; every new member must complete a "democracy workshop" to get a grounding in both cooperative values and process;

members are urged to attend and be involved in every board and staff meeting; and a network of twenty "stewards" exists, independent of the board and the managers, to assist members with problems and serve as mentors.

Our society does not teach people to work together (these days, even in elementary school, kids are pushed to get ahead of all the others, to seek competitive advantages, to "beat" the kid next to them). Yet here's a business that is achieving success in the marketplace, not by getting people to set aside their egos, but by motivating them to combine their egos in a constructive effort for the good of the entire group. Union Cab Cooperative shows that self-management works, that it's not some 1960s dreamworld but a sensible, powerful way to organize the creativity, energy, and ambitions of workers outside the hierarchical corporate model. "It might not be the prettiest way to run a company," said McNamara, "but it works out to be the best way."

CHAPTER 6

The Good Business Life

What if businesspeople started saying no to success? I mean "success" as measured by the frenetic corporate culture: Become the biggest! Devour your competitors! Get superrich! Win!

What if, instead, there were calmer, saner models of business success based on a more measured pace of life and the achievement of broader human needs? Well, there are!

Paul Marshall, a management professor at Harvard Business School, noted a recent trend of entrepreneurs rejecting the conventional path of zooming from start-up businesses to far-flung, mega-growth conglomerates. "Many small companies simply don't want to get bigger," he reported. "I talked with the owner of one company who had a chance to buy out a competitor and decided against it. He told me, 'I'd rather pack my kids' lunch and walk them to school.' He just felt his life was a lot better if he stayed small."

Andrew Field ran a sizable printing company in Minneapolis. In 1987, however, he gave it up and moved to a small town on the banks of Montana's Yellowstone River—not for a business opportunity, but for "a simpler life." Since then, he's built a new printing business named PrintingForLess.com, focused on old-time values of customer service and a team spirit among employees. Field said that his goal is to make the "publishing experience a more pleasant one for everyone." It seems to be working. As one longtime customer enthused, "We've had the same team of [PrintingForLess] people for years, and I know them all on a first-name basis. We're partners."

The people who are choosing such a heretical business path are still out to make a profit, just not a killing. They want more control over their own lives and want to build businesses based on genuinely satisfying their customers, treating workers as valued partners, and being a personal, contributing presence where they are.

CONFUSED ON THE CONCEPT

A man who lived with his wife on a Caribbean island was visited by a type A friend from New York. "What is it that you do here all day?" asked the New Yorker.

"Oh, not all that much," replied the laid-back islander. "I get up around ten, read the paper, and have coffee on the beach. After that, I take my boat out to fish for a couple of hours. I sell my catch at the market, but my wife and I keep some to eat for lunch. In the afternoon, we just enjoy each other's company, read books, go for a swim, and maybe take a nap. Then we usually stroll into town to have drinks and dinner with friends, listen to some local music, and get to bed around midnight."

"But don't you see you're missing an unbelievable business opportunity here?" asked the visitor. "With all this fish, you could get a fleet of boats, open a processing plant, move to New York to handle distribution, and make a fortune!"

"Yeah, I guess so," said the islander, "but I'd have to give up this place."

"No, you wouldn't," retorted his friend. "With the money you'd make, you could come down here on vacation every year and just chill out for a couple of weeks."

Arsen Avakian, for example, runs a small chain of tea shops in Chicago, but he's not dreaming of a franchised "Avakian Empire" of ten thousand tea shops from coast to coast. "You need to become part of the community and give people an alternative to the big chains," he said. "When I go to Starbucks, I ask for a latte, and instead of hearing 'Thank you,' I hear 'Next.'"

Smaller, simpler, more personal.

These qualities are not extraneous to the profit goals of American business; they are integral. Cambridge Naturals, a neighborhood grocery just down the street from Harvard Square, does very well, despite having to contend with three Whole Foods supermarkets within two miles and two other groceries in the Square itself. Co-owners Michael Kanter and Elizabeth Stagl have had several chances to open other stores around Boston but prefer to do business in their own special way. Kanter said, "[Americans] live in an isolated and lonely culture. When you ask people what is missing from their lives, it isn't a big-box store. People stop in to our store for the social interaction as well as the products. We're an oasis."

TO YOUR HEALTH

Chris Johnson is a thirty-five-year-old pharmacist in Austin, Texas. He had worked for nearly a decade in chain-store pharmacies and was doing well, pulling down nearly $100,000 a year and gliding along an upward career path. But, he said, "It made me sick to my stomach."

He was sickened by the outrageous prices being charged and by the burden this put on folks who had no insurance coverage, and he had this to say about it:

> These drugs are bankrupting people. I saw too many instances where people had to make hard decisions between keeping on the electricity and keeping their hearts in the right rhythm. Too many instances of patients walking away from the counter because of the simple fact that they could not afford their medications. And my hands were tied by the corporations for whom I worked. I couldn't lower the prices for these people, even though I knew how much the drugs really cost us and that the profit margins were obscene.

Another sickening factor was that he did this twelve hours a day, putting in six-day weeks. Yeah, there was a nice paycheck, but he came home to a dark house every night, with all of his family asleep. He barely saw his wife, Bryna, and their two sons. Inside the corporate system, he could neither do what he wanted to do nor be who he wanted to be. "There has to be a better way," Chris said to himself at the time.

And now there is, because he created one. In April 2005, Johnson opened what he calls "our unique little pharmacy," naming it MedSavers.

Unique, indeed. "Now," said Johnson, "I'm back doing what I went into pharmacy to do—helping people." MedSavers caters to those who have no health insurance or whose meager plans don't cover the cost of prescriptions. He dramatically lowers the prices for his customers by selling only generic drugs and by cutting overhead to a bare-bones level. He and Arturo Herrera, a medical technician, are the only full-time employees. Plus—and it's a big plus—MedSavers does not deal with insurance corporations, so Johnson saves time, money, and agony by not having to wrestle with the paperwork of those enormous, nay-saying bureaucracies.

Even though this is only one small pharmacy, with none of the wholesale buying clout of, say, the five-thousand-store Walgreens chain, MedSavers delivers serious savings, typically charging only half as much as the big boys do.

Johnson noted that he sells ninety capsules of the generic version of Prozac for $15.80, while CVS charges $58.99 for the same thing. "I could add another $20 on my price and customers would still think it's a good deal, but I'd be getting into the same mind-set as the chains. There's a business model of 'charge as much as you can,' but I like the business model of 'charge a fair price'—what you need to keep yourself in business and take care of your family. I'm all for making aprofit—and we do—but I have a problem with obscene profits, whether it's a pharmaceutical company, a retail drugstore, or a shoe-repair shop."

The price that Chris pays for ethics is that he no longer makes $100,000 a year. "But, you know, people don't really need as much as they think they do," he said. "It's a matter of aligning your work with your values."

Even though he works hard, Johnson deliberately set the hours of his pharmacy at ten to six on weekdays and nine to two on Saturday, so that he and his employees can have a life. "I can now have breakfast every morning with our two boys, and I'm home in time for dinner and bedtime with them," Johnson explained.

Also, work itself is more of a pleasure. He's come to know the people he serves, not by their prescription numbers but by name. He shoots the breeze with them, learns about them and their families, and builds community right into his business.

Then there's the satisfaction of knowing that your work matters. MedSavers not only has customers, but ones who are deeply appreciative that someone gives a damn whether they can get the medicines they need at an affordable price. "To go home and feel I made a difference in somebody's life is a huge, huge thing," said Johnson, beaming.

STRIPPING DOWN THE WORKPLACE

Owners are not the only ones yearning to improve their quality of life by reorganizing the workplace to suit them; workers are doing it as well. In the North Beach area of San Francisco, for example, a group of women were getting no respect from the owner of their business . . . until they decided to take matters into their own hands.

These are the women of the Lusty Lady Theater, one of scores of strip clubs that line the streets of the Broadway district in North Beach. Angry about being treated like chattel, the real-life ladies of the Lusty Lady decided to turn their anger into action. In 1997, sixty dancers and fifteen of the support staff did something unheard of: they joined the Service Employees International Union, turning their place into the nation's first unionized strip joint.

They might dance naked for a living, but these women showed that they have the smarts, gumption, determination, and unity to gain better pay, basic worker rights, and a measure of dignity in an industry that offers none. In fighting for workplace democracy, however, you don't simply win union recognition and that's it. You have to stand your ground, stay alert, and expect the unexpected.

In 2003, the unexpected hit the strippers' union hard. After winning six contentious contract battles and improving their working conditions, the ladies suddenly learned that, nonetheless, they were to be tossed into the street. Rather than respect the union, the owners decided just to shut the place down. There were no other strip club owners who wanted to take on a union club, so that was that.

Once again, though, the ladies were being underestimated.

"We can just take it over," said Delinqua, one of the dancers. Indeed, the union members had talked about this possibility before, and now they were forced to turn the possibility into reality. "We had become a strong group, we had gotten used to working together, and we just believed," said Ruby. For help, they called on friends at a couple of successful cooperatives in the city and quickly decided that the way to go was to organize themselves as a worker-owned, unionized co-op.

The strippers weren't without necessary skills. Some had college degrees, a couple were in graduate schools, one had been a lawyer (she said that practicing law made her "feel like a whore," so she made a career move), and all were street savvy. For example, Miss Muffy, a twenty-two-year-old high school dropout, plugged into the Internet and figured out how to write a legal contract for the group. She commented that "sometimes people just try to mystify their profession. It didn't seem that difficult."

Everyone took assignments. Pepper negotiated the purchase with the owners. Miss Muffy signed people up as co-op owners, Ruby dealt with the city, Havana handled the incorporation process, Rapture and Cayenne wrote bylaws . . . and so forth.

As chronicled by Bay Area writer David Steinberg, the Lusty Lady became an exercise in democracy building. Any of the workers can become co-op owners for $300 (payable on the installment plan to make it affordable to all). At the end of the year, profits are divided among co-op members, prorated on the basis of hours worked. Decisions are made by majority vote, but they try for consensus so that everyone's concerns are included. Dance evaluation, which used to be done by the managers who were not dancers themselves, is now done by a team of five dancers, with members of the team changing every week. Financial matters are open for all to see—how much money came in and what checks went out are posted weekly.

"Before this, I didn't know anything about business," said Ruby. "We're all learning accounting procedures, about insurance—things I never thought I'd be doing when I signed on as a stripper."

CHAPTER 7

Banking on Change

It's hard to feel much fondness for bankers. "Soft-hands people," they were sneeringly called by my uncle Emmett, who'd been a small farmer, a long-haul truck driver, and a ranch foreman—a rough-hands guy who never got the time of day from the money minders.

And today's banks are worse: conglomerated, automated, out-of-state, faceless fee-grabbers with all the warmth of their ATM kiosks. When the Wells Fargo megachain took over a bank in my neighborhood, the first thing it did was take down the electronic sign that gave us locals (gave, as in, *for free*) the time and the tempera-

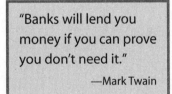

"Banks will lend you money if you can prove you don't need it."

—Mark Twain

ture, replacing this small symbol of neighborliness with its own red-and-gold logo. These far-flung financial empires are happy to take your money, but if you want real service or need a loan, you'd better be a "premium customer."

A small-business fellow I know, who had banked at the same place for years, watched as his bank went through its third or fourth merger and noticed that everyone working there was now young, new to town, and didn't even know his name, much less anything about his business. Exasperated by the cold indifference he got from them, he walked into the lobby one day and shouted, "I want to talk to somebody with a pulse!"

BANKERS WITH A PULSE

What if there were a bank that actually gave a damn about local people, about small business, about helping to build equity for locals in their own community—as well as about its own profitability? Welcome to ShoreBank!

In 1973 Chicago, there was a neighborhood that pretty well defined "blight." South Shore, close to Lake Michigan, covers about 250 blocks. In the early seventies, the neighborhood had blocks of empty storefronts, boarded-up buildings, weed-choked lots, and low-income renters.

White flight had drained South Shore of many of its businesses, and the city's banks were redlining the whole area, refusing to make home loans or invest business capital in this "undesirable" neighborhood (now consisting mostly of African American families), even though the banks collected deposits from the people living there. Like a giant vacuum, banks were sucking capital out of the community where it was most needed and transferring it to places where it was least needed but could deliver the greatest return to the bankers. With no investment, the South Shore community was withering and had lost hope for the future.

Then something positive happened, although it seemed like a negative at first. South Shore National Bank, right in the vortex of the blight, was bleeding money. Having lost $35 million' worth of deposits in four years, the owners applied to federal regulators for permission to abandon the neighborhood and relocate to Chicago's prosperous downtown.

But South Shore's residents rebelled, asserting that the abandonment was racially motivated. The feds agreed—and, for the first time in U.S. history, a bank was not allowed to relocate just because its neighborhood demographics had changed.

The community won this important procedural battle, but seemed destined to lose its bank nonetheless. Since the owners were losing deposits and no longer wanted to be in the neighborhood, they put the bank up for sale. Good luck—who in their right mind would buy into such a losing situation?

Meet Milton Davis, James Fletcher, Ron Grzywinski, and Mary Houghton. In the 1960s, these four had worked together in one of America's first small-business loan programs for minorities, and they'd become friends, sharing a passion about finding how best to deal with such declining neighborhoods as South Shore. They were convinced by experience that traditional approaches on their own couldn't work because the programs and the groups didn't have the resources and the staying power to make a lasting difference and really change these neighborhoods. As bankers, they grasped one fundamental reality: for any community to be vital, it must own its own capital assets (businesses and homes), not just be renters, consumers, and workers for absentee owners.

In conventional banking terms, their idea that a commercial bank, flanked by strong community-development organizations, could effectively restore South Shore *by investing in the people themselves* was unheard of.

So, they bought the bank.

Making It Work

Using banking to lift up a neglected, decaying neighborhood was completely against the conventional wisdom of both liberals and conservatives. "No one thought we could succeed in South Shore," said Grzywinski. "What we were trying to do was a unique idea. Informed people thought there was no way it could work."

Of course, scientists still say that physiologically and aerodynamically, there's no way a bumblebee can fly, so pay no attention to "informed people." These bankers did not, and they pushed through the doubters to buy the bank. "You can't start something like this without believing that you will succeed, no matter what," Ron said. Mary added a caveat: "We were always sure we were going to persist and succeed. Of course, we were sure a good decade before we were certain."

They patched together $800,000 from a couple of wealthy investors, dozens of supportive individuals, the United Church of Christ, and a host of foundations, plus they scored a $2.4 million loan from the American National Bank in Chicago, whose officers knew Ron's banking history and trusted him. Unlike all the other bankers, who had redlined the neighborhood, these four looked at what was in front of them and saw something big that others had missed: assets!

First, even though many of the residents were low income, people there had bank accounts that collectively added up to millions of dollars. The problem was, this neighborhood capital was being deposited in branches of the big uptown banks and invested God

---

A BANKER NAMED BILL

In contrast to Bank of America, Citibank, and the other sprawling giants, Western National Bank in Phoenix has one location. One. It doesn't even have a drive-through facility. But it does have what the huge outfits do not: style, personality, and happy customers.

Instead of a drive-through, Western has a roadside "drive-up." At the bank's curb, a valet teller stands at a cobalt-blue counter, shaded from the Arizona sun by a big umbrella, taking deposits. Every customer is handed a receipt . . . and a bottle of springwater. Children are given toy safes. There's also a courtesy courier service to pick up deposits from the bank's small-business customers.

Western's owner, William D. Hinz II ("Call me Bill"), is the direct opposite of the impersonal megabanks. "Customers want to be greeted by name and treated as though their $2,000 savings accounts or $50,000 small-business loans really matter," he said. "Our customers absolutely love it."

knows where. Reverse this capital outflow, and the community could be in a position to "greenline" itself.

Second, while many of the buildings were run-down three-story walk-up apartments, the structures themselves were solid. South Shore had an enormous stock of housing that was just waiting for rehab, transforming ugly ducklings into swans. Third, the people of South Shore turned out to have untapped skills and entrepreneurial energy. They knew carpentry, masonry, plumbing, wiring, woodwork, and other crafts, and many were fledgling businesspeople. This was not a community looking for charity. It was a community needing an opportunity.

The bankers went to work. They reached out to the residents to convince them that their neighborhood had a future and that the bank would invest in them. In addition to attracting local depositors, the bank sent solicitations throughout the country to progressive individuals, groups, and businesses, asking them to put some of their funds into "Development Deposits" at ShoreBank and promising both a competitive rate of return and that the funds would be invested directly in the regeneration of the community.

Money came, and the bank put it to work, making loans to local folks to buy and refurbish apartment buildings. As all banks do, ShoreBank issued FHA-insured loans, but it also risked the bank's own capital in projects—a strong signal to the community that it was there to stay.

Loans were not merely flung out to anyone who walked in the door. Remember, these are bankers, and the key to the sustainability of their vision is that the projects succeed, the loans are paid back, and profits are made. "We spend a lot of time with our borrowers," said Houghton. "We want to know that they can do the job and manage a building or run a small business."

Building by building, the community started to believe (even absentee landlords were happy, for rather than just letting their property deteriorate—or torching it for the insurance money—they now had a way to sell it). To show faith, the bank remodeled and landscaped its own building. It also created a nonprofit community-development arm to seek funding for community groups, programs, and services.

Expanding the Vision

By 1975, the bank was profitable, and South Shore was on its way to its present transformation as one of Chicago's most vibrant neighborhoods, filled with good homes, thriving businesses, and community spirit.

The bank began to replicate its development approach in 1986, opening ShoreBank branches in the inner cities of Cleveland and Detroit. Some children on Cleveland's east side are now benefiting from this expansion. They are a mix of black, Anglo, Latino, and Asian kids who attend a unique day care school owned by Tammy Newsome-Rawls. She wanted to create an innovative center that introduced children to multicultural experiences at an early age, while also giving them broad educational instruction.

Despite having excellent credentials, fifteen years of experience, and a good business plan, Tammy was turned down for a loan by two traditional banks because she didn't have the collateral and the cash to cover the amount banks were willing to lend (confirming, once again, Mark Twain's point). At ShoreBank Cleveland, however, she found a whole different attitude. "They have a loan department strictly for day care!" Tammy marveled. She got a start-up loan of $85,000 and opened the doors to the Allemas Child Care and Enrichment Center in 2005. "It was a blessing," she said. In only two years, Rawls has added three thousand square feet to her center and doubled the number of children she's serving.

In the mid-1990's, big things happened for ShoreBank. First, it doubled in size to just over half a billion dollars in deposits when it merged with a minority-owned bank in Chicago. Then, a whole new chapter began when the bank teamed up with an innovative nonprofit called Ecotrust, based in the Pacific Northwest. With this partnership, ShoreBank became the first banking corporation in the United States to put environmental issues at the center of its lending policies, as it tried to build a bridge between conservation and economic development.

SAVING ENERGY, SAVING MONEY

Andre Bennett came to ShoreBank seeking a rehab mortgage for his Southside Chicago home, which was sorely in need of fixing up. He got more than he expected.

The bank had just started its first-in-the-nation "Homeowners Energy Conservation Program." Andre immediately got a free energy audit of his home to see what was needed to make it energy efficient. Then he was offered a package that rolls the conservation costs right into the rehab loan, which makes the energy fix more affordable. Bennett said, "They showed me how adding extra insulation and choosing energy-efficient windows and appliances would lower my utility bills by nearly 30 percent. In Chicago, that's no small thing."

It opened ShoreBank Pacific in Ilwaco, Washington, and Portland, Oregon, focusing on loans to organic farms, Native Americans, and fishing enterprises. It also created "EcoDeposits" for these banks, drawing depositors nationwide who get a market rate of return on their money while seeing their funds invested directly in local businesses that reduce pollution and waste, use energy efficiently, and conserve natural resources.

In 2000, the bank extended its environmental lending to all locations and became a pioneer in giving comprehensive mortgages that include making conservation improvements in the home to save energy. The borrowers are able to cut their utility bills dramatically, recouping their investment in only three to four years.

The Triple Bottom Line

Young people looking for a career that might allow them to express their social values and create a better world rarely think of banking. In fact, many Americans have a soft spot in their hearts for bank *robbers*, sensing a sort of populist justice in that line of work.

But here's living proof that the power of money can be harnessed to serve the greater good, if only you have the vision and the determination to broaden the possibilities. ShoreBank is a model for doing that, defining banking success in a way that encompasses three bottom lines: profitability, community development, and conservation. The numbers speak for themselves:

- Since its 1973 beginning, ShoreBank has financed the purchase and renovation of 52,000 affordable residences.

- Just since 2000, it has loaned more than $318 million in loans to small or minority-owned businesses in its targeted communities.

- In 2006 alone, it made more than $202 million in conservation loans, $365 million in community development loans, and $134 million in loans that did both.

- Overall, during its 30-plus years of existence, it has invested more than $2.9 billion in underserved communities.

- It has 494 employees, 71 percent of whom are African American; 45 percent of its officers are minorities, and 30 percent of its senior managers are women (including the president).

- Meanwhile, at the end of 2006, ShoreBank had $2.1 billion in total assets and enjoyed $5.2 million in profit.

The bank's slogan is "Let's Change the World," and it's doing its part by viewing people as assets and giving them opportunities to pursue their dreams. "We do not accept the world as it is," said the founders. "We recognize value where others may not."

Connections for Part One

Are you interested in businesses that are different and that make a difference? Businesses that are grounded in progressive values and based on a broader vision than grabbing all the money they can? The following sources will provide you with everything you need to know, from how to support such enterprises to how to start one of your own. Many of these groups can supply materials, models, advice, how-to tips, hands-on help, and inspiration.

The first grouping consists of companies, co-ops, networks, unions, and banks that we mentioned in this section of the book, listed here in order of their appearance. The second group contains additional entities that support independent business efforts and/or challenge corporate chains and conglomerates that are crushing small enterprise.

Institute for Agriculture and Trade Policy
2105 First Avenue South
Minneapolis, MN 55404
Phone: (612) 870-0453
E-mail: iatp@iatp.org
Web Site: www.iatp.org

Peace Coffee
2801 21st Avenue South, #120
Minneapolis, MN 55407
Toll-free: (888) 324-7872

E-mail: info@peacecoffee.com
Web Site: www.peacecoffee.com

Cooperative Coffees, Inc.
302 West Lamar Street, Suite C
Americus, GA 31709
Phone: (229) 924-3035
Web Site: www.coopcoffees.com

Organic Valley Family of Farms
CROPP Cooperative
One Organic Way
LaFarge, WI 54639

Phone: (888) 444-6455
Web Site: www.organicvalley.coop

Earth Dinner
E-mail:earthdinner@organic
  valley.coop
Web Site: www.earthdinner.org

**U.S. Federation of Worker
  Cooperatives**
P.O. Box 170701
San Francisco, CA 94117-0701
Phone: (415) 379-9201
E-mail: info@usworker.coop
Web Site: www.usworker.coop

Grameen Foundation
50 F Street, NW
Washington, DC 20001
Phone: (202) 628-3560
Web Site: www.grameenfounda
  tion.org

**Dunn Development
  Corporation**
Martin Dunn
151 Seventh Avenue, 2nd Floor
Brooklyn, NY 11215
Phone: (718) 388-9407
E-mail: info@dunndev.com
Web Site: www.dunndev.com

Hidalgo Medical Service
Charlie Alfero
530 DeMoss Street
Lordsburg, NM 88045
Phone: (505) 542-8384
Web Site: www.hmsnm.org

Patagonia
259 Santa Clara Street
Ventura, CA 93001
Phone: (805) 653-0798

Union Cab—Madison
P.O. Box 8305
Madison, WI 53708-8305
Phone: (608) 242-2010
Web Site: www.unioncab.com

Net Impact
88 First Street, Suite 200
San Francisco, CA 94105
Phone: (415) 495-4229
Web Site: www.netimpact.org

MedSavers
Chris Johnson
3810 Medical Parkway #115
Austin, TX 78756
Phone: (512) 465-9292
Web Site: www.medsaversrx
  .com

Printingforless.com
Andrew Field
100 PFL Way
Livingston, MT 59047
Phone: (800) 930-6040

Argo Teas Inc.
Arson Avakian
16 West Randolph Street
Chicago, IL 60601
Phone: (312) 873-4123
Web Site: www.argotea.com

Cambridge Naturals
Michael Kanter and Elizabeth
  Stagl
Porter Square Shopping
  Center
Cambridge, MA 02140
Phone: (617) 492-4452
Web Site: www.cambridgenaturals
  .com

Lusty Lady Theatre
1033 Kearny
San Francisco, CA 94133
Phone: (415) 391-3991
Web Site: www.lustyladysf.com

Service Employees International Union (SEIU)
1800 Massachusetts Avenue, NW
Washington, DC 20036
Phone: (202) 730-7000
Toll-free: (800) 424-8592
Web Site: www.seiu.org

ShoreBank
7054 S. Jeffery Boulevard
Chicago, IL 60649
Phone: (800) 669-7725
Web site: www.shorebankcorp.com

Also at the following locations:

540 East 105th Street
Cleveland, OH 44108
Phone: (216) 268-6100

14533 Mack Avenue
Detroit, MI 48215
Phone: (313) 642-5200

ShoreBank Pacific
721 NW 9th Avenue, Suite 195
Portland, OR 97209
Phone: (503) 916-1552

ShoreBank Pacific
203 Howerton Way, SE
Ilwaco, WA 98624
Phone: (360) 642-1166

Western National Bank
Bill Hinz
2525 East Camelback, Suite 100
Phoenix, AZ 85016
Phone: (602) 553-7444

Connect with these groups, too:

American Independent Business Alliance
222 South Black Avenue
Bozeman, MT 59714
Phone: (406) 582-1255
E-mail: info@amiba.net
Web Site: www.amiba.net

Helps locally owned businesses to organize alliances to support and promote their enterprises, providing tools, tips, and good ideas for small businesses that are trying to contend with the power of absentee-owned chains and conglomerates.

BALLE (Business Alliance for Local Living Economies)
165 11th Street
San Francisco, CA 94103
Phone: (415) 255-1108
E-mail: info@livingeconomies.org
Web Site: www.livingeconomies.org

An alliance of businesspeople in the United States and Canada with fifteen thousand members in fifty-two cities. BALLE provides tools, business models, and other resources to local businesses; creates opportunities for businesspeople to network and share their best practices; encourages local purchasing; maintains an online marketplace of community-based businesses; and advocates public policies to strengthen local businesses.

Co-Op America
1612 K Street NW, Suite 600
Washington, DC 20006
Phone: (800) 584-7336

Web Site: www.coopamerica.org

A national support group for cooperatives, with an emphasis on environmental sustainability. Provides tools and advocacy for co-ops, while also promoting green shopping (publishes an annual directory of products and services called *National Green Pages*), social investing, and community investing.

Corp Watch

1611 Telegraph Avenue #702

Oakland, CA 94612

Phone: (510) 271-8080

Web Site: www.corpwatch.org

Educates and mobilizes people on issues of corporate accountability including human rights violations, environmental degradation, and corruption. Good source of information for students, teachers, and activists.

Global Exchange

2017 Mission Street

San Francisco, CA 94110

Phone: (415) 255-7296

Web Site: www.globalexchange
.org

A spirited human rights organization that takes on everything from global trade scams to environmental justice. Its innovative efforts include annual GreenFests showcasing the products and ideas of hundreds of green enterprises (cosponsored with Co-Op America), selling a large line of fair trade goods from artisans and craft co-ops in forty-two countries, and conducting "Reality Tours" to various countries.

Institute for Local Self-Reliance

1313 5th Street Southeast

Minneapolis, MN 55414

Phone: (612) 379-3815

Web Site: www.ilsr.org

A research and advocacy organization that works with local governments and businesses to develop, expand, and protect the economic health of their independent, sustainable enterprises. Also, runs a "Hometown Advantage" program that helps local folks beat the big box megachains and chart a new course for democratic economic development in their communities.

Ohio Employee Ownership Center

113 McGilvrey Hall

Kent State University

Kent, OH 44242

Phone: (330) 672-3028

Web Site: www.dept.kent.edu/oeoc

While it focuses on Ohio, its models, research, technical assistance publications, databases, and networking lists are a good starting point for anyone who wants to explore the feasibility of employee ownership of a business.

Program on Corporations, Law and Democracy (POCLAD)

P.O. Box 246

S. Yarmouth, MA 02664-0246

Phone: (508) 398-1145

E-mail: people@poclad.org

Web Site: www.poclad.org

A democracy movement that provides historical background, current information, tools, resources, and assistance to politically active citizens who are trying to challenge corporate power in their communities and even challenging the very idea of corporate personhood.

Social Investment Forum
1612 K Street NW, Suite 650
Washington, DC 20006
Phone: (202) 872-5361
Web Site: www.socialinvest.org
Provides guides, advocacy, and networking for organizations and individuals who want to put their savings and investments into enterprises that are socially and environmentally responsible, while also earning competitive returns. Runs a joint membership program with Co-Op America Business Network that offers direct services to members.

Social Ventures Network
P.O. Box 29221
San Francisco, CA 94129-0221
Phone: (415) 561-6501
Web Site: www.svn.org
A network of successful entrepreneurs who want to help other businesspeople do well by doing good and focusing on developing new models and leaders for both socially and environmentally sustainable businesses. Holds numerous forums and events around the country, provides peer-to-peer learning sessions, and offers a useful online information source called "Tools and Best Practices."

Sprawlbusters
Al Norman
21 Grinnell Street
Greenfield, MA 01301
Phone: (413) 772-6289
E-mail: info@sprawl-busters.com
Web Site: www.sprawl-busters.com
Helps local community coalitions to design and implement campaigns against the encroachment of megastores. Provides consulting services on topics that range from strategic planning to technical support. Its online directory lists more than three hundred communities that have waged successful campaigns, offering background information about each fight.

United for a Fair Economy
29 Winter Street
Boston, MA 02108
Phone: (617) 423-2148
E-mail: info@faireconomy.org
Web Site: www.faireconomy.org
Provides extensive research and action tips (often creative and fun) on such broad issues as tax fairness and America's widening class divide. Helps local communities to develop strategies and organize to democratize their own economies.

Wakeup Wal-Mart.com
1775 K Street NW
Washington, DC 20006
Phone: (866) 253-1350
Web Site: www.wakeupwalmart
   .com

A national campaign that is working to change the corporate practices of this abusive retail giant. The Web site provides links and action items so that ordinary citizens can fight back effectively; these items range from simple letter-writing efforts to an "Adopt-a-Wal-Mart" program.

Wal-Mart Watch
1730 M Street NW, Suite 601
Washington, DC 20036
Phone: (202) 557-7440
Web Site: www.walmartwatch.com

A citizen's research and action group that challenges the bullying tactics of the world's biggest retail corporation. Its "Battle-Mart" program is an active online guide for local people confronting Wal-Mart; it provides battle plans, tips, case histories, and contacts.

PART TWO

POLITICS

"People often say with pride, 'I'm not interested in politics.' They might as well say, 'I'm not interested in my standard of living, my health, my job, my rights, my freedoms, my future, or any future.'"

—Martha Gellhorn, novelist and renowned war correspondent

CHAPTER 8

Shape Up, America!

It is fashionable in Washington's political watering holes for various campaign consultants, pundits, and lobbyists to gather in circles of cynicism, sip martinis, and make snide remarks about the American electorate—the great unwashed, the hoi polloi. . . aka you and me.

> Voters are as dumb, lazy, and submissive as a bunch of cud-chewing cows. They can be herded down any trail we choose for them, as long as we promise a ration of corn to eat and a block of salt to lick.

Of course, these numbskulls don't know diddly-squat about regular people, but guess what? They don't know anything about cows, either. In particular, they're willfully ignorant of the rebellious spark that exists within all of us creatures. Let us tell you the story of the Feral Cows of Cheeseboro Canyon.

Few animals are perceived to be as docile as your average bovine, which seems content to spend its short life standing in a field, eating, mooing, and pooping—before being led to slaughter. So, imagine the surprise of people in Southern California to learn that a renegade herd of at least nine wily cows are loose in the canyons, oaks, and brush of the Santa Monica Mountains National Recreation Area.

Some seven years ago, these Jersey and Angus cattle broke free of their pen on the Ahmanson Ranch, disappearing down into Cheeseboro Canyon, located in the adjacent park. You would assume that it wouldn't be much of a cowboy challenge to track and recapture a band of cattle mooing as they roam through a public park that's popular with hikers and bikers, just across I-405 from Beverly Hills. The *Los Angeles Times* even ran a tongue-in-cheek wanted poster to help find the livestock (see below).

Yet for seven years, these sirloins on-the-hoof have avoided the efforts of park rangers and others to round them up. In fact, they're rarely seen.

How can this be? Well, get ready for a surprise. Animal scientists say that even slow-moving, slow-witted, domesticated farm animals have a born-to-be-wild streak they never really lose. If they escape confinement, their naturally wild survival instincts can kick in.

So, these once-sedentary and obese cattle quickly adapted to their new environment. They slimmed down to a wiry physique, became more agile, and turned savvy enough to outwit and outmaneuver those trying to corral them. Park ranger Jim Richardson is one of the few who has laid eyes on the herd: "I came close to them, and they just took off running like a deer might if you were to get too close."

Richardson said that they might even be reproducing. He believes that by now, this elusive, cunning, self-governing herd has moved out of the park onto adjoining lands—staying wild, defying their captors . . . and still roaming free.

We can be the cud-chewers that the power elites think we are, docilely going along with the politics we're given. Or we can break loose and help to build a new politics based on our democratic ideals and our aspiration to be self-governing. To get there, we must reassert the noble notion of political involvement.

What is politics?

> *(Again with the "what is!" What's with you, DeMarco? And you, Hightower? Here's a better question for you: Do you two think we're stupid? Politics is the BS they do in Washington. It's city hall, which you can't fight. It's the big shots with the money buying both parties. It's the lobbyists and the corruption and the stink. You think we don't know what goes on? Lemme tell you, those in charge don't give a tobacco spit about us regular people. Where's the honest politician who's gonna save us? The game is fixed. Count me out. I don't want nothin' to do with no politics.)*

Then you're going to be a cud-chewer, albeit one who whines a lot. Remember this: if you're not involved in politics, others are. That means you're leaving basic decisions about your life to them. Things like war, pollution, health care, taxes, pensions, education, middle-class opportunities—all are left to what today is a rather small minority. Yeah, the current political system is rotten, but we can't be idiots about it.

By "idiot," I don't mean stupid. I mean the original Greek word, *idiotes*, referring to those who refused to take part in public decisions—which is to say, politics. The Greeks gave us that word, too. Actually, it comes from two Greek words: *polis*, meaning the community of citizens, and *politeia*, which means conducting the business of the community. In the Greeks' ideal system, citizen involvement in the community's business was not limited to elections but was extended to every aspect of the people's public life, to all things that concern us as a society.

I'm sure you're grateful for that little lesson in Greek civics, but let us put it to you in blunt English: **Shape up, America!!!** Come on, get a grip—recognize where you are, who you are, and what you have to do. This is the U.S. of A., you're a citizen, and if you really want America to be a self-governing nation, then you have to take responsibility for making it so.

Helloooooo . . . Knock-knock . . . Anyone home? *Self*-government means just what it says. The selves are you and me—and you and you and you. We have to *do* the governing. Yes, that takes some effort, it takes some time, but—Yoo-hoo!—that's what it means to be a democracy.

Start with this reality: the Powers That Be don't want genuine democracy. They don't want you and me included in self-government, for that would stop their kleptocracy. They intend for politics to be a spectator event for us, scripted by the one-tenth of 1 percent of elites who put up the controlling money. They want you to be a consumer of the junk-food politics they create: Here you go, boys and girls, watch the clever ads we've made for you. Then you get to vote for your favorite among the fine candidates we've preselected for you. That's the American way, boys and girls. Can you say, God bless America?

Sure, that makes most people cynical, angry, and disgusted. So the almost-irresistible temptation is to say, "The hell with it" and drop out. Of course, that's exactly what the elites are aiming for. Every person who surrenders his or her role as a self-governing citizen becomes a bystander and gives the grinning hyenas of power one more degree of control over our society.

New bumper sticker: "Don't Be a Bystander, Be a Stander-Upper!"

Too many progressives keep waiting for progress, as though someone's going to come along and generously hand power over to us, hand over health care, peace, a clean environment, and all the other essentials of a good life. It won't happen. Never has. Yet DeMarco and I are often asked questions like: Why can't we have a new New Deal? We need a real progressive to be president—who do you think can do that? Why doesn't Congress save us from Bush? When will we win? Should I move to Canada?

Snap out of it! No one can do it for us. It takes all of us being willing to do what we can over a long period of time, persevering, connecting with one another, bucking one another up . . . and laughing as we go, enjoying the fight. This is what democracy is—ordinary people standing up, speaking out, adding others to the cause, and not ducking the hard work as we make incremental gains.

> "When trouble arises and things look bad, there is always one individual who perceives a solution and is willing to take command. Very often, that individual is crazy."
>
> —Dave Barry

Even when we "win," we can't back off because you can be damned sure that the forces of plutocracy and autocracy will be burrowing upward like crazed weasels to reclaim their privileges and power. (*Relevant digression*: A sign in a mall in Beijing, China, warning of a wet floor, said in English: "The Slippery Are Very Crafty!" I suggest that these signs be posted throughout the halls of Congress and the White House).

Americans recently got a taste of the craftiness of the slippery. It followed the 2006 congressional elections, which had been such a jolt of joy for us progressives. Among other clear messages this election sent to Washington, the American majority (including hordes of disgruntled Republicans) had shouted in unison that they were appalled by the TomDeLayJackAbramoffDukeCunninghamBobNey scandals and wanted the corrupt link between lobbyists and lawmakers severed. Period.

We were all heartened when the new House Speaker, Nancy Pelosi, flatly declared in January 2007, "The American people voted to restore integrity and honesty in Washington, D.C., and the Democrats intend to lead the most honest, most open, and most ethical Congress in history." Sure enough, the first thing the Democrats did was to outlaw lobbyist-paid junkets for Congress critters, ban free jet travel aboard corporate jets, and forbid other freebies. That was wonderfully refreshing . . . for a few days.

The glorious glow of reform did not even last through the month of January, for lobbyists and lawmakers quickly found the loophole in the law: direct corruption is out, but indirect is in. Under the reform, influence peddlers can no longer pick up the tab to fly Representative Slippery to the Super Bowl, put him up in the finest hotel, honor him at a private party, and let him watch the game for free in the host corporation's luxury skybox.

Ready? Here comes the big *but*: crafty lobbyists can simply put a big wad of money into a special political committee set up by Representative Slippery. Then, technically, that committee pays for the

---

JACK THE GRIPPER

Superlobbyist Jack Abramoff was King of the Grin and Grab style of fund-raisers for members of Congress. These are typically held at swank Capitol Hill restaurants and hosted by a power broker like Jack. They're quickie affairs—the lawmaker simply strides over from the Capitol, grins and shakes hands with a roomful of lobbyists bearing $5,000 checks, has a libation or two, scarfs down some paté and crab balls, grabs the money, and goes.

Abramoff had such a full schedule of these (morning, noon, and night) that he finally decided to open his own restaurant, Signatures, to handle all the traffic.

lawmaker's Super Bowl weekend, plus he gets to keep what's left over to use in his next campaign, pay for other junkets, and so forth. Sweet! It's like having your reform and eating it, too!

Just in the first month of the new Congress, Senator Max Baucus offered lobbyists the chance to go skiing, snowmobiling, or golfing with him in Montana. Price per lobbyist: $5,000, payable to his political committee. Senator Mel Martinez of Florida invited lobbyists to spend quality time with him during a weekend trip to Disney World at $5,000 a pop. Others came up with such creative events as "Manicures and Muffins" at a Capitol Hill nail salon, a delightful evening on Broadway to see *Mary Poppins*, and a martini night at a D.C. steak house. My personal favorite was a bargain deal from Representative Eric Cantor. For $2,500, a lobbyist could join Eric for coffee at Starbucks on four different mornings in the spring (it's unclear whether he charged extra for scones).

> (*See, right there's exactly what I'm talking about! The people spoke, and the bastards in Washington just laughed at us. What's the use? You know, pals, you should never try to teach a pig to sing. It wastes your time and it just annoys the pig. I give up.*)

Well, poor baby! Thank goodness you weren't around at the founding of our country, when standing up for democratic ideals meant more than the occasional discouragement; it could also lead to the confiscation of your property and cost you your life. And what about the workers of the last century who were clubbed and shot for daring to stand up to the bosses, or how about the unbelievably courageous people of the civil rights movement who were hung, bombed, mutilated, and burned alive in the segregationist Jim Crow years, while Congress looked the other way?

Suck it up, friends. Sure, today's Congress and the Bushites are stiffing democracy—they shuck and jive, bob and weave, duck and hide while 75 percent of Americans want real lobbying reform, 77 percent want the United States out of Iraq, 66 percent want the government to guarantee health care for everyone, 87 percent want the feds to negotiate with drug companies to lower the price of prescriptions, 69 percent want the government to guarantee food and shelter for all, 76 percent believe there is too much power concentrated in the hands of a few corporations, 65 percent say corporations make too much profit and put profits over the public interest, 83 percent want stricter regulations to protect the environment, 69 percent want more emphasis on fuel conservation than on developing new oil supplies, 68 percent say labor unions are necessary to protect working people, and 74 percent are concerned that corporations are collecting too much personal information about people.

It's disappointing and infuriating that both the White House and Congress are stiffing us, but look who's on the short end of those numbers! Not you and me. Not the progressive cause. We have big majorities with us. Those who are stiffing these popular reforms are the ones with a numbers problem, and our job is to keep pressing the issues. In fighting for truth and justice, remember this: if at first you don't succeed, you're running about average.

You might be glad to know that good folks like you are battling the bastards, democratizing the process, and making fundamental political gains from coast to coast. These are regular people who're simply refusing to be passive as the moneyed set assaults our country's democratic aspirations. They are involved in both direct electoral politics and the development of our grassroots political base. In every case, they are fighting for their ideals and making a difference, while having a good time doing it—and so can you. Read on!

CHAPTER 9

Run for It!

Americans have a great sense of humor, and if you don't believe it, look at whom we elect to office. Even I got elected—not once, but twice, to statewide office in Texas.

In fact, Texas is rich in the politically ridiculous (it's a point of pride for us, actually). We elected a guy named Jesse James nine times—as our state treasurer! Ma Ferguson, elected governor here in 1924, opposed a bill to provide bilingual education, declaring, "If the King's English was good enough for Jesus, it's good enough for me." You want smart pols, go elsewhere. Or look at our infamous Tom DeLay, who has claimed that God chose him for high office. (I know that the God of the Old Testament is portrayed as vengeful and wrathful beyond all comprehension, but could any deity be that mean?)

We can't blame God for who's running our government. We've done this to ourselves, mostly by default. What's happened is we've let the moneymen, the consultants, the ad buyers, and the power brokers be our choosers, allowing them to abandon the grassroots for a centralized politics of money and media. Without grassroots politics, it's hardly surprising that elected officials feel little loyalty, responsibility,

---

FOOT POWDER FOR MAYOR

America has elected some real doozies to office—rubes, thieves, perverts, nutballs, incompetents, liars . . . even dead people.

So far, though, we've not elected a foot powder, as the people of Picoazá, Ecuador, did in 1967. A company selling a foot deodorant named "Pulvapies" ran an ad during the mayoral election: "Vote for any candidate, but if you want well-being and hygiene, vote for Pulvapies."

When the votes were counted, the Honorable Pulvapies had been written in as the people's choice.

---

or even ties to regular folks. And if the system has no ties to grassroots people, why would they feel any ties to the system?

I think you can see the downward spiral of democracy here: money decides the election outcome, the elected officials side with money over the interests of the people, the grassroots turn off, the candidates hug money ever tighter . . . and away they go.

So, it's hopeless, right? Nonsense! This is America! People can be knocked down, dissed, and dismissed, but then they figure it out and come up with ways to push back, to reinvigorate their inherent democratic zeal, and to start reclaiming power. Contrary to what today's elites would like us to believe, you can run against them . . . and win! To see this revival in action, let's take a bus ride.

GET ON THE BUS

Rebellions are often conceived, nurtured, and developed in bars. In fact, during the rebellious founding of our nation, taverns were known as the "headquarters of the revolution." So it is appropriate that a loose group of politically frustrated young Oregonians gathered at the Rogue Brewery in Portland late in 2001 to talk about fomenting a little rebellion in the politics of their state.

Oregon, with a long tradition of progressive public policies and politicians, was suffering from a bad case of creeping right-wingism.

For a decade, the state had been beset by a double-barreled Republican legislature. These members were not from the Teddy Roosevelt school of GOPism but the Newt Gingrich foam-at-the-mouth, antigovernment, pro-corporate branch. For example, the public education system, a point of tremendous pride in Oregon, was being taken apart by the legislature's religious extremists and privatization ideologues. Also, lawmakers had been taking a chain saw to the conservation laws that had carefully protected the state's invaluable natural beauty, turning these public resources over to the whims of profiteers, even though polls showed that this was not at all what the people wanted.

The young folks who were quaffing brews and making notes on cocktail napkins that evening were not "political" people in the usual sense—none held office, worked in politics, or were politically connected. But they were concerned citizens, and they wanted things to change. The question was: What could they do?

Several ideas were tossed around at the get-together, but one guy seemed to have the closest thing to an actual plan. Jefferson Smith, a twenty-something lawyer, had done the political math. He reported that while the state House was divided 35–25 in favor of Republicans and the Senate was 16–14 Repubs, a significant number of the GOP lawmakers came from suburban and rural districts where they were winning elections by very slim margins—in a half-dozen House races, their margin of victory was only a couple hundred votes each.

"Let's get out of Portland!" Smith exclaimed in a eureka moment. What if hundreds of young volunteers were to go to these swing districts to help progressive candidates? Flip a couple of seats in the Senate and six or so in the House, and the whole state agenda changes.

Yeah, let's go! But where? How? To do what? "None of us knew what we were doing, what we were biting off," Smith admitted later.

Next came more sessions in bars and at kitchen tables to enlist others, plot a strategy, and raise some money. Funding is always short in these grassroots ventures, so an ability to scrounge is essential. The initial group kicked in some funds, hit up some friends and family members, and soon got a reputation for throwing cool parties to raise cash. Also, with this being a volunteer enterprise, expenses were kept low, and the group learned to live off the land.

Still, they needed someone to coordinate the chaos, and Joe Baessler was conscripted to be the first full-time employee (even today, with a much larger operation, there are only a half-dozen paid employees). Baessler, who'd recently graduated from law school in Michigan, had moved to Portland in 2001. Unemployed, he met Smith and liked the "impossible dream" aspect of Smith's political idea, so he signed up for the job at a fat salary of $800 a month.

At first, funds were so tight that Baessler had a hard time getting reimbursed for cash he had laid out to get the office up and running. He kept pleading that his thin personal finances were stretched to the breaking point, but no money was forthcoming. Finally, Smith showed up at the office and said, "Here, Joe, I've invested in a cell phone for you," which was really just a sop to hold Baessler in place until a few more bucks were raised. Baessler laughs today that the real reason for the "gift" was that it allowed Smith to reach him at any hour and give him more work to do.

From the start, everyone agreed that to engage young volunteers, the effort had to be different . . . and fun. This led to the notion of the bus. It began as a mundane discussion on how to transport volunteers to the districts. "We'll just rent a bus," said Smith. "You know," chimed in Charles Lewis, "you can buy one a lot cheaper than you can rent one."

Okay, our own bus! That's cool. Where do we get one?

Turns out there's a bus store! Not a Buses 'R' Us, exactly, but Smith's dad, Joe, knew a mechanic who knew a guy out in Spokane who sold used buses. A call was made, Joe and his mechanic friend flew out to kick the tires, and, for $11,000 (loaned to the group by Joe), they drove back to Portland in a forty-seven-seat, 1978 charter bus.

This gave them more than wheels—it gave them a name: the Oregon Bus Project. Just quirky enough to cause people to ask, "The what?" It also gave them a symbol connected to the inspiring history of Rosa Parks and the Freedom Riders (and reminiscent of the freewheeling spirit of Ken Kesey, with maybe a little Willie Nelson thrown in). Plus, it provided a big, visible, mobile presence, physically representing democracy in motion, while offering volunteers the bonding experience of what the Bus Project calls "community in a

---

THE KITZHABER DENT

In May 2003, just before the first bus trip, the Oregon Bus Project persuaded the good progressive governor at the time, John Kitzhaber, to do the honors of christening the bus with a bottle of champagne. It did not go smoothly. He whapped the bus on the designated spot. Nothing. The bottle didn't break, but it did dent the bus, which has an aluminum body. So the Guv whaled away at it two more times. No success, except to deepen the dent (which remains to this day the "Kitzhaber Dent"). Finally, he broke the bottle on a lug nut.

---

vehicle." The bus even gave the Oregon Bus Project a slogan for getting people to join the effort: "Get on the Bus!"

This was politics that did not seem off-putting, intimidating, hierarchical . . . dull. "We knew that most of our friends weren't spending their time going to political party meetings," Smith said. "We needed to make politics a piece of people's social lives." Sasha Pollock, who was drawn to the Oregon Bus Project by its antiestablishment attitude, likened it to livening up C-SPAN with some MTV: "It's not just making it fun, but you make it accessible to people who mostly see established politics as something foreign and not open to them."

Caitlin Baggott, who was one of the first trip organizers, said: "A question we're asked all the time is 'How do you do it? How do you get these young people involved?' And I think the answer is really simple: You ask them!" Another key for the Bus Project was that it was not about a political party but about values and ideas, engaging young people to make a difference in moving Oregon and the country in a progressive direction. It was welcoming, fun, idealistic, and important—four elements that appeal to young people . . . and to people of all ages, for that matter.

But would they really come?

The kickoff trip was scheduled for June 15, 2002. The Bus Project had contacted a couple of Senate candidates in suburban districts who said, "Yeah, if you can bring us a few kids to go door-to-door with us on Saturday, that'd be swell." The organizers flung out a net to activist groups, circles of friends, and colleges, asking for volunteers. They also made use of something that, at the time, was new to politics—e-mail—creating the first political e-mail list in the state. "We had no idea if this was going to work, whether we'd get ten people or fill up the bus," said Baggott. She got to the staging area at seven in the morning, hung the big "Get on the Bus" banner, put out the coffee and doughnuts—and hoped. A car arrived, then another . . . and finally more than 150 people rolled in. The only ones more pleasantly surprised than the organizers were the candidates. "They didn't really expect us to come through," Baggott said.

The Oregon Bus Project quickly gained some serious political buzz, and candidates began to call them, putting up a few bucks for gas money and supplying food. On a typical trip, the bus and the accompanying caravan of cars may pull into, say, a school parking lot in the targeted district, to be greeted by the candidate and a throng of local supporters. Garrett Downen, now the managing director of the Bus Project, said that the local folks usually erupt in cheers as the entourage arrives, "because here comes the cavalry."

The candidate gives a pep talk, basic ground rules are covered (don't walk on people's yards, etc.), and the volunteers fan out in fours

---

DOOR-KNOCKING FUN

What's the one night every year that you expect people to come knocking on your door? Halloween! And Halloween is always just a few days before the election. So the Oregon Bus Project launched a "Trick or Vote" event, with volunteers in costume going door-to-door in targeted districts to urge folks to turn out on Election Day. Afterward, everyone would come together for a party. In 2004, about eight hundred people went trick-or-voting with the Oregon Bus Project—the biggest voter-canvassing event in state history.

to work blocks that are determined by the local campaign. "I was scared out of my gourd to actually talk to voters," said Downen, who, like most of the participants, had never done it. "I mean, this isn't normal. But that's why it's so wonderful, because when you talk to someone, they're surprised you're doing it, that you actually made the effort." But isn't it disheartening to get doors slammed in your face? "You get almost no door slams," Smith said. "You get many, many more people who say, 'Thank you for talking to me.'" People might be conservative, added Downen, but "you've got something in common. They're worried about health care; you're worrying about the same thing. If you just go out and say, 'Hey, I met a candidate this morning who wants to make a difference for us in the legislature, who'll be fighting for us, and here's how. This is why I'm giving up my Saturday and doing this for free!' That really resonates with folks."

Making trip after trip into numerous suburbs, down the Oregon coast, into the hard-hit timber communities, out to Deschutes County, and elsewhere, the Bus Project has brought thousands of new people into politics, knocked on hundreds of thousands of doors, and had an impact that those who met in the Rogue Brewery six years ago would not dared to have imagined. Let's mark it in bold:

- In the 2002 and 2004 elections, the Bus Project focused on the Senate, targeting a total of ten races. **Their candidates won nine**, taking control of the Senate out of right-wing hands!

- In 2006, the Bus Project turned to the House, targeting races in ten swing districts. Again, **their candidates won nine**, moving the House out of right-wing control!

The impact goes beyond legislative realignment to the personal. The Oregon Bus Project's approach empowered ordinary people to be the difference makers. The Bus Project bought no ads, hired no consultants, and did no mass mailings or auto-dial phone calling. It was all volunteer power—face-to-face, honest, doorstep politicking. It was enormously invigorating for the volunteers because each person could truly sense that his or her participation mattered.

Pollock pointed to the Bus Project's 2004 effort for Jeff Barker, who won in his suburban district by only forty votes: "We went out three times for him and brought probably three hundred people total out there. Each person would knock on more doors in a day than forty, so each one could have been the difference. It's a really inspiring thing to go, 'I helped with this. I'm not the only drop in the bucket, but I was a drop.' And without every drop, the bucket would not have filled up to overflowing."

The Oregon Bus Project is meaningful combined with fun. Smith cited the project's Rule Number 1: "Take the subject matter seriously. Don't take ourselves seriously." Corollary Rule Number 1B: "If it's not

---

DEBATES

Woody Allen said that anyone who does not believe in eternity has never spent an evening with an insurance salesman. I'd add that an evening watching a political debate can be just as excruciating—media dullards asking inane questions to non-responsive political dullards in an interminable bore-a-thon.

The Oregon Bus Project, however, has done the impossible by juicing up this tedious ritual into something you'd pay money to see. They call it Candidates Gone Wild (CGW), a "debate" that brings contenders for various offices together in a sort of game show format. Cosponsored by Portland's largest independent paper, the *Willamette Week*, this thing's a hoot. It includes a *Jeopardy!* quiz-show segment, a Donald Trump–style "You're fired" segment, and a candidate's talent show at the end. Bush-Kerry boring it's not.

The beauty is that CGW takes the stuffiness right out of politicos, liberating them at least momentarily from their stilted, on-message, campaign personas. They still get to explain their stands on issues, but in a way that's improvisational, more candid, and certainly more enjoyable than mouthing their practiced platitudes. Everyone, including the candidates, has a great time, and people literally do pay to see it, filling the eleven-hundred-seat Roseland Theatre all three times it's been held.

a little bit silly or funny or irreverent, we should probably rethink it." Every bus trip ended with a party, a potluck, or a community hurrah of some sort, with people sharing stories, sipping some cool ones, and making the political convivial.

Asked what advice he would give to someone who's thinking "Hey, maybe I should get some buddies together and start something like this in our state," Smith replied, "Go immediately to the nearest mental institution and have your head examined." (Actually, he said no such thing. We threw that in just to say that this ain't tiddlywinks; it's a real commitment with lots of difficulties. We now return you to the story in progress.)

Here are two pieces of advice that Smith did offer:

1. Be results driven, not process driven. Pick an objective, then go out and get it done. Victories matter, especially in volunteer efforts. It's very energizing for people to say, "Wow, we did this." They might even show up again!

2. Decide to do it. "The most important thing for us," Smith said, "was that we made up our minds we were going to do this. That was more important than how much money we had, 'cause we didn't have any. It was more important than how much political expertise we had, 'cause we didn't have any. The most important thing was that we decided to do something."

CHAPTER 10

Clean Elections

Our friend Molly Ivins collected tales of the Texas legislature, pulling out a little gem from time to time to regale a visitor with an anecdote of pea-brainedness, moral turpitude, ideological zaniness, or just raw ignorance. Here's one of her classics about the corrupting power of money in politics.

A state senator from west Texas took $200 from a lobbyist to support a certain bill. But, astonishingly, when the bill came up, the senator voted against it! The betrayed lobbyist caught up with the backstabber outside the Capitol and laid into him good, demanding to know why he'd gone back on his word. "The other side offered me $400," confessed the senator. This caused the lobbyist to explode all over the guy. "Well," said the senator, with offended dignity, "You knew I was weak when I took the $200."

Unfortunately, the occasional bribee is not the real problem. It's the system of American politics itself that's weak, hooked on ever-increasing injections of cash, which makes our public agenda dependent on those who deal in big political money. It's an inherently corrupting, self-perpetuating, virulently antidemocratic system in which private money buys multiples of public money. Here's the schematic:

> *Start.* ➡ Private interests (overwhelmingly corporate) invest millions of dollars in select candidates. ➡ These favored ones get elected (in 95 percent of congressional races, the candidates with the most money win). ➡ The grateful recipients push the corporate agenda (to the exclusion of other agendas), delivering billions of dollars to the campaign investors through special tax breaks, subsidies, no-bid contracts, regulatory favors, and other public benefits. ➡ Corporate lobbyists become the fund-raisers for those officeholders who deliver for them. ➡ *Return to start.* ➡

This is not merely the pay-to-play system of Tom DeLay, Duke Cunningham, Jack Abramoff, and others who've been caught reaching too brazenly into the goodie bag—it is also the system of those not yet caught, of those who play the system with a lighter touch, including some who speak loudly of the need for reform (as long as "reform" doesn't go so far as to interrupt the cash flow).

Thus we had the mysterious case of "The Disappearing Populist Mandate of 2006." In that year's congressional elections, even voters in many Republican districts tossed out powerful incumbents, clearly saying they were sick of business as usual in Washington. Among the issues prompting this nationwide voter revolt were the war, health care, drug-company price gouging, and Big Oil's assorted rip-offs.

Take the latter. Oil corporations have had such a gusher of profits that the chief of ExxonMobil said in 2006 that he didn't know how the company could possibly spend it all. The public, however, had a suggestion: 80 percent of Americans (including 76 percent of Republicans) favored slapping a windfall profits tax on these greedheads and putting the money into developing alternatives to oil.

Of course, Washington refused to do any such thing. In fact, Congress and the White House let these bloated giants siphon tens of billions of dollars from our public treasury in special tax breaks they did not need and often weren't even meant to get. "Holy Huey Long," protested many of the Democrats running in 2006, "This is an abomination!" They thumped the tub hard, promising that they'd push to repeal all of these giveaways. "Hooray!" shouted voters.

Early in 2007, these spirited new Democrats in Congress seemed to have the backing of Speaker Nancy Pelosi, who publicly called for a "rollback" of Big Oil's $32 billion in subsidies. All this populist fervor had the industry's lobbyists trembling in their Guccis and muttering to one another. But then, money spoke.

Old-school, corporate-minded Democrats in Congress said, "*Tsk-tsk*, now, let's cool down. If we're to keep control of Congress and win the White House in '08, we're going to need our friends in Corporate America writing checks for our campaigns." Next thing you know, a dozen key Democratic lawmakers and about twice that many of the industry's lobbyists (including those representing every major oil corporation) gathered together for a private tête-à-tête to review the proposed legislation.

> **"I've got so many new friends these days."**
>
> —Representative Charles Rangel, the new head of the tax-writing Ways & Means Committee, after twice as many lobbyists as expected showed up at a January 2007 fund-raiser for him

Shortly afterward, Pelosi put forth and passed her rollback bill . . . which itself had quietly been rolled back from $32 billion in cuts to—guess how much?—$5.5 billion! That's not a cut, it's an emasculation! Rather than bold action in response to public demand, the party let Big Oil slip away with $26 billion' worth of tax subsidies— our money!—tucked in its back pocket.

> *(See, it's hopeless. Haven't I been telling you two that? Republicans sell out, Democrats sell out. Forget about trying to change the system. There's way too much money at stake, so nothin's gonna clean it up. You reformers are just a bunch of wheel spinners, getting people all bothered about something they can't do anything about. Go find some honest work to do.)*

THE CLEAN SOLUTION

Sure, it's hopeless if you're just going to crank back in a La-Z-Boy and wait for Washington to bring reform to you. Instead, look to the states and cities, where you'll find good people rolling up their sleeves to do the honest work it takes to change the system. They're showing us all how to reclaim our government from the clutches of the moneyed interests.

Their reform mechanism is a rather simple notion called clean elections (CE). Here's the essence of it: CE is a voluntary system that gives candidates for state and local offices a clear choice: (1) go ahead and run the old way if you want, ceaselessly hustling campaign money from private funders and hocking your independence to them; or (2) choose to forego money from private interests (and from your personal wealth) in return for receiving no-strings-attached *public funds* to finance your campaign.

CE candidates receive a fixed and equal amount of public money. They get an allotment to run in their party's primaries (including third-party primaries), and those who win receive another allotment for the general election. Also—and very important—if a CE candidate is being grossly outspent by a candidate with Big Bucks backing or one spending a personal fortune, the clean candidate gets an extra allotment of matching funds to stay competitive.

It works! Six states (Arizona, Connecticut, Maine, New Jersey, New Mexico, and North Carolina) and two cities (Albuquerque and Portland, Oregon) now have some form of public financing in place . . . and the results are phenomenal.

Candidates across the board—Democrats, Republicans, Greens, Independents, Libertarians, and others—have chosen to run clean, rejoicing that doing so liberates them from the necessity of going around incessantly rattling a tin cup for donations. It has also meant that more women and people of color are running and winning, more incumbents are being ousted (including in the primaries), more issues are seeing the light of day, and more people are paying attention to elections . . . and to voting. In other words, CE is changing politics.

How's this for change? Maine has had four legislative elections since its public-financing option took effect in 2000. The results are stunning: *83 percent of Maine's state senators and 84 percent of its House members have now been elected without turning to corporate*

REGULAR PEOPLE

Deborah Simpson was a single mom waiting tables in a Maine restaurant in 2000. Being paid half the minimum wage, plus tips, Simpson was hardly the sort of well-connected person who gets elected to the state legislature, but there she is. With clean elections, she said, "it was doable." Now in her fourth term, Simpson brings working-class issues to the legislature that were ignored in the past because there were no elected officials with the ground-level viewpoint of a waitperson.

Serving with her is Nancy Smith, a Maine farmer first elected in 2002 against a lobbyist-backed opponent. She did not know anyone in the money circles and had no time to go hustling campaign funds, for she has chickens to feed and cows to milk. "Clean campaigns allow those who work to run for office," Smith said, "and they create 'citizen legislatures.'"

interests to finance their campaigns. Just as striking, in Arizona, ten of the eleven statewide officials, including the governor and the attorney general, have been elected as clean candidates.

These electoral earthquakes are fundamentally altering the political landscape, and they are being generated by ordinary people like you who are fed up with money politics. Yes, it takes effort, time, gumption, and perseverance. But the payoff is rich: you matter again in the political realm. Yes, it means encountering the fierce opposition of the political establishment. Still, you can win. Don't underestimate how much power plain ol' citizens actually have if they get organized behind a good idea.

That's what happened in North Carolina in 2000, when a coalition of Tarheel groups, assembled under the banner of North Carolina Voters for Clean Elections (NCVCE), determined to break the iron fist of money in state politics. Rather than trying to get public funding for every state office at once, however, they decided to take one step at a time and prove that such a system would work and be popular with voters and candidates alike. Their target: the state's two top courts.

It seems an odd choice at first, but the seven-member Supreme Court and the fifteen-member Court of Appeals were making decisions on everything from corporate cases to legislative redistricting that—to put it mildly—called into question the impartiality of justice. In a statewide poll, a large majority of voters (and 72 percent of black voters) agreed with this statement: "There are two systems of justice in North Carolina—one for the rich and powerful and one for everyone else."

These judges are elected, and they were drawing the bulk of their campaign funds from corporate interests and powerful law firms that had cases before the courts. Not only did this money put special-interest judges on the bench, but it also created a money barrier that nonconnected candidates were unable to hurdle.

To liberate justice from the cold grasp of campaign cash, the coalition pushed a bill in the legislature calling for Voter Owned Elections in these court races. There was support from many lawmakers, but Republicans in the general assembly locked arms with corporate lobbyists, pledging to kill it. This was not something that could be won inside the capitol, where money holds sway. So NCVCE moved the battle outside the assembly, going to the countryside to rally broad public support for the reform.

For two years, the coalition (which included voter leagues, churches, students, democracy activists, civil rights organizations, businesspeople, teachers, labor, and taxpayer advocates) organized a series of home-district constituency meetings that drew thousands of North Carolinians into face-to-face sessions with their legislators on this issue. A little creativity also helps a cause, and the coalition came up with some clever ways to reach wavering legislators:

- Schoolteachers were enlisted to telephone their former students who were now in the assembly. ("Hi, Bobby, it's Ms. Wilkinson from Jefferson High, calling to see if you remember anything I taught you in that history class thirty years ago. Don't make me have to come to Raleigh to set you straight, you hear?")

- Yard signs are nice, but location is everything. So, undecided legislators suddenly found that their own neighbors were prominently displaying yard signs in favor of the reform.

- When six of the seven Supreme Court justices opposed the bill, NCVCE produced a bipartisan list of thirteen hundred respected attorneys and judges in the state who favored it, including all thirteen of the previous thirteen presidents of the North Carolina State Bar Association.

- To say "hello" to recalcitrant Republicans and counter their obstinacy, a GOP polling firm was commissioned to take a survey, revealing that 70 percent of the party's voters supported the pubic-financing option.

The grassroots troops trekked to the capitol in September 2002 to cast watchful eyes on their lawmakers, who were about to vote on the Judicial Campaign Reform Bill. It was a squeaker in the assembly—57–54 in favor—with one Republican joining the majority. Five days later, the Senate approved it 34–12.

On October 10, Governor Mike Easley came to the old House chamber for a joyous signing ceremony. The chamber was packed

---

THE PEOPLE SPEAK

It's common for opponents of public financing to dismiss it as a Big Government intrusion that people don't want. But in 2006, a bipartisan national poll asked voters whether they would support public financing of congressional elections.

- Seventy-four percent said yes, including 65 percent of Republicans.

- All age groups, genders, and regions supported it—most of them by about 75 percent majorities (none by less than 60 percent).

- Eighty-two percent said that public funding means candidates will win on ideas, not on money; 81 percent said that politicians will be accountable to voters, not to large donors; and 77 percent said that special interests will not receive as many favors and insider deals from officeholders.

with reformers, legislators, and a few curious tourists. But the most amazing sight was up in the gallery seats, which were filled with eighth graders specially invited to the event. Can you imagine? Inviting innocent children to watch a law being enacted!

Then it was time to put the reform to the test. In 2004, two Supreme Court seats and three Appeals Court seats were up for election. Clean candidates took both seats on the Supreme Court and two of the other three. Big Money was pushed to the back; special interests put up less than 14 percent of the judicial funds that year, as opposed to 73 percent before the reform.

In 2006, another six seats on these courts were up for grabs, and the publicly financed contenders won five. Four of these clean-election winners were women, including Patricia Timmons-Goodson, the first African American woman to be popularly elected to North Carolina's top court, and Sara Parker, elected as chief justice.

Instead of merely being agitated about the corruption caused by money, you can start agitating and do something about it. Clean elections can come to where you are . . . if you help bring them. They can be applied to any level of political campaigning you choose, including governors, legislators, judges, county offices, mayors, councils, school boards, water districts—even your local hog inspector.

FOLLOW DORIS

Take heart from the story of our friend Doris Haddock, better known as Granny D. This petite great-grandmother from Dublin, New Hampshire, was genuinely, deeply outraged by the scourge of money-soaked politics in America. How could she leave such a foul political inheritance to her grandchildren? Rather than sit and seethe, Doris wanted to make a statement, to *do something*. But who was she? What could one person do?

"I'll walk," she decided. Not down to town hall—across America! The whole of it. At eighty-nine years of age, this seemingly delicate lady donned her emblematic straw hat, unfurled her banner calling for publicly financed clean elections, and set out on foot from Pasadena, California, on New Year's Day 1999. Destination: Washington, D.C. For fourteen months, Granny D. traversed our country, walking ten miles a day, day in and day out, lifting hearts all along the way.

She weathered 105-degree deserts, a close call with a tornado, and a blinding snowstorm. She kept going. She encountered a rattlesnake in Texas and Senator Mitch McConnell in Kentucky. She kept going. She gave speeches at rodeos and in legislative chambers. She kept going. She had to have her feet taped sometimes to walk and she wore a steel corset to help her back. She kept going.

DeMarco and I kept up with Granny all along the way, featuring her on the *Chat & Chew* syndicated radio show we did at the time. Throughout her journey, we visited with her on the air nearly every Friday, getting updates on her adventures, health, and spirit. The day she entered Washington and walked to the Capitol (passing right up Lobbyists' Row on K Street), we broadcast the moment live. Our listeners *loved* her, loved both the anger and the hope that she represented, loved her message.

"Along my three thousand miles through the heart of America, did I meet anyone who thought that their voice as an equal citizen now counts for much in the corrupt halls of Washington? No, I did not. Did I meet anyone who felt anger or pain over this? I did indeed, and I watched them shake with rage sometimes when they spoke, and I saw tears well up in their eyes. The people I met along my way have given me messages to deliver here. The messages are many, written with old and young hands of every color, and yet the messages are the same. They are this: 'Shame on you, senators and congressmen, who have turned the headquarters of a great and self-governing people into a bawdyhouse. The time for this shame is ending. The American people see it and have decided against it. Our brooms are ballots, and we come a-sweeping.'"

—Doris "Granny D." Haddock, speech from the Capitol steps
at the end of her walk, February 29, 2000

She's become the Matron Spirit of Democratic Reform, inspiring people in cities and states all across the country to join her rebellion. Now ninety-eight, Granny is still a force. A couple of years ago, corporate lobbyists in Arizona were going to try to repeal the state's very effective clean election law. Granny D. flew into Phoenix and held a press conference, not merely to scold the perpetrators of this regression, but to promise that she would return at election time to walk the districts in opposition to any legislators who supported repeal. With that, all of the air went out of the lobbyists' proposal. None of the members would touch it, for they didn't want Granny coming after them.

Now, we must do the walking. It's even possible for us to force Congress to get off the dime and provide the clean-election alternative for its seats. Every state and city that passes its own reforms shows that it works and that people support it, putting upward pressure on Congress to come clean, too. This will take a while, but more than a hundred current members of Congress have already declared their support, so it's not out of reach.

At whatever level, clean elections are a prize that's worth the fight, for they provide a path for ordinary voters to take our government back and start moving forward.

A TRIP TO KANSAS

Unfortunately, not all political movement is forward, since there are always forces of ignorance and arrogance loose on the land, trying to pull us backward. In the late 1990s, the people of Kansas had their own *Wizard of Oz* moment, causing many to mutter the line Dorothy said to her little dog: "Toto, I've a feeling we're not in Kansas anymore."

Kansas had been turned into a Land of Oz when a band of "intelligent design" extremists cranked up their election machine behind a curtain of moral righteousness. Running as Republicans, they seized control of the state board of education. Next thing you know, the board was spewing out vast plumes of pseudoscientific smoke, trying to camouflage religious beliefs as science.

What had happened? At the time, there was much pontificating by pundits that the good people of Kansas had collectively made a hard right turn, embracing the vindictive, self-righteous agenda of such extremist Christian political fronts as the Moral Majority and Focus on the Family.

Wrong. As in so many states, Kansans had largely quit paying attention to such low-visibility races as those for the state school board. It's dangerous in a democracy for people to avert their eyes because that's when narrow special interests can assert themselves in a very focused effort and slip into power, causing a state to lose its way in a hurry. In short order, Kansas became a battleground of hot-button politics, pitting the "intelligent design" right wing against Charles Darwin and the scientific community.

In 2005, a 6–4 "creationist" majority of the state board rewrote the standards for teaching science in the public schools, essentially denying that evolution exists and mandating that its brand of religious dogma be peddled to Kansas schoolchildren as literal truth.

> "I was a Republican until they lost their minds."
>
> —Former basketball star Charles Barkley

This made the state a punch line for late-night comedians— amusing for the rest of the nation, but Kansans didn't care to have themselves caricatured as know-nothings or to have their state pitched into a divisive political standoff. The Pat Robertson/James Dobson branch of political religion used Kansas as a rallying cry, a model of what it hoped to impose on the rest of the country. Even George W. felt obliged to add his intellectual weight to the conflagration, allowing as how "intelligent design" and the "theory" of evolution should be given equal emphasis in the classroom. The tone got ugly. When science teachers protested that you could believe both God and Darwin, the religious zealots branded them "worse than atheists." One of the extremists on the state board showed the depth of her thinking by declaring that evolution was "biologically, genetically, mathematically, chemically, metaphysically, wildly, and utterly impossible."

For a while, Kansas was lost in the darkness. But, then, flicker by flicker, the light of sanity began to reassert itself. Yes, most Kansans tend toward Republicanism, but not toward nutballism. This is also a state with a hearty populist history and a modern reputation for levelheadedness and sensible discourse. It's full of rational people who were not going to bow meekly to a repressive order, even if that order wore the robe of theocracy and waved the Bible as its "authority."

The first rebellious breakthrough came only three months after the creationist board imposed its will on the public schools. The town of Manhattan, out in farming country, rose up against the edict. By a 6–0 vote, the local school board rejected the teaching of "intelligent design" in its science classes.

Next came a big change. You would not have seen this news in the national media or heard about it on the comedy shows, but in 2006 the real Kansas stood up. In that year's election, five seats on the state board of education were up for grabs. Darwin himself was not on the ballot, but nonetheless he won three of the five seats. Two of the intelligent designers got bounced in their own Republican primary, ousted by moderates who said that religion belongs in religion classes, not in a science curriculum.

THE WRATH OF PAT

In November 2005, the voters of Dover, Pennsylvania, booted out eight school board members who had injected an "intelligent design" program into their school district's science curriculum, replacing them with pro-evolution candidates. This unleashed the hellacious wrath of Pat Robertson on the poor denizens of Dover.

"You just voted God out of your city," intoned the pompous televangelist. He predicted that a calamity would befall them and said they should expect no heavenly relief: "If there is a disaster in your area, don't turn to God; you just rejected him." Instead, the apocalyptic absurdist advised with a demonic smirk, "If they have future problems in Dover, I recommend they call on Charles Darwin."

The rebellion had even carried over into other statewide races. Two lifelong Republicans, appalled that the zealots had hijacked their party, switched parties in 2006 and were elected lieutenant governor and attorney general as Democrats. Lieutenant Governor Mark Parkinson, who once had been the Kansas Republican Party chairman, said, "I got tired of the theological debate over whether Charles Darwin was right. I'm not spending the rest of my life on that issue."

On February, 13, 2007, the new 6–4 majority of the education board voted out the religious standards, returning the science of evolution to the school children of Kansas. Coincidentally, the vote came the day after Charles Darwin Day, which celebrates both his birth and the date in 1859 when *On the Origin of Species* was published. Dorothy and Toto were back in Kansas.

CHAPTER 11

Democracy School

We know what average Americans think of politicians—but what do politicians think of us?

One clue is that numerous politicos turn out to be quite touchy about touching the masses. Ironic, huh? But true: many of those who make their living as gladhanders really aren't that pleased to be shaking our hands. Germs, you know.

Take Dick Cheney. At a 2006 fund-raising event in Topeka, the Republican faithful lined up to shake hands with the veep. Before reaching him, however, they had to get past a lady who stood adjacent to Cheney holding a big bottle of Purell, a sanitizing lotion that promises to kill "99.99 percent of most common germs." To get their grip and grin with the honoree, every guest had to accept a squirt of the goop to purify their hands! Then, once the line had passed, Dick ducked backstage to rub a generous dollop of the antiseptic into his own hands, thus cleansing himself of the contact he'd just endured with the great unwashed.

Contrast this sort of prissy politicking with our friend Paul Wellstone. We knew the late senator and his wife, Sheila, and can tell you that he absolutely reveled in one-on-one, press-the-flesh contact with the body politic. (*One tidbit*: Senatorial decorum fit Paul worse than his rumpled suits. Other solons of the upper chamber can get a little huffy about protecting their special perks, such as having senators-only elevators to ride in the Capitol. They always hated getting on the elevator with Paul because of his penchant for holding the door open for any gaggle of tourists standing there. To the consternation of his colleagues, he would gleefully wave the commoners on board to ride with the senators.)

(*Okay, one more tidbit*: Not long before Paul died, I was scheduled to do a morning radio interview from the grounds of the Minnesota State Fair. I arrived early and wandered off to find a cup of coffee. I darted into one of the food halls that dot this huge fairground, and as I reached the counter, a gleeful voice shouted out from across the room, "Jim Hightower!" It was Paul. He'd been there since the 7 a.m. opening, greeting people and sitting and visiting at length with whoever walked in for a bite of breakfast. Members of the public were not prescreened by security and no staff person was there to run interference for Paul. He was just a senator hanging out with the folks.)

When Paul, Sheila, their daughter, Marcia, and three staffers were killed in a plane crash in northern Minnesota in 2002, not only did America lose a progressive champion who connected at a gut level with ordinary people, but the progressive movement also lost one of our few elected officials who (1) understood the political necessity of organizing a grassroots base, (2) knew how to do it, and (3) intended that this effort not merely build a base for him, but empower regular people to take charge of their politics, *their* democracy.

His people-centered approach did not fit today's conventional political wisdom, which considers vacuousness to be a virtue. "All we have to do to win is rake in plenty of money to burn on TV ads and make sure our candidate doesn't get in the way or say anything unscripted," the experts explain. It's the "Karl Rove Doctrine," although Democratic consultants worship at the same altar. Imagine, then, how ridiculous the national Democratic establishment thought Paul was to insist on building a big volunteer base and actually training them. "Did anybody see his spaceship land?" they snickered. Yet he was twice elected to the Senate against big-money Republicans and was about to win again when that damn plane went down.

Consultants don't even like yard signs, which at least give a campaign the pretense of having a grassroots program. Put all your money into media is their "wisdom"—yet Paul put 40 percent of his campaign budget into a ground-level effort. This is unheard of in U.S. Senate races. The result was that he had *five thousand active volunteers* working throughout Minnesota. That's not five thousand names shoved into a forgotten computer file somewhere, but five thousand ready-to-go activists who had been trained, who had specific jobs to do and knew how to do them. This was citizenship in action, and it's powerful enough to beat money.

Paul is gone, yet he lives in the form of a dynamic organization named Wellstone Action, launched in St. Paul in 2003 by his former campaign manager, Jeff Blodgett, along with Paul and Sheila's two sons and a group of longtime supporters. It is a national democracy school that travels throughout our country to teach local folks the skills and provide the knowledge they need to organize around an issue, to head up a campaign, or to run for office.

Wellstone Action's approach is a bit like that of a wonderfully helpful store here in our town of Austin, Harrell's Hardware. The people of this small business are down-to-earth friendly, they know what they're doing, they're willing to help you figure out how to tackle a project, and they'll even loan you a tool to do the job! Harrell's slogan is "Together We Can Do It Yourself."

That could be the motto of Wellstone Action. "Our democracy depends on people being involved," said Blodgett, "and we try to help them do it successfully." The centerpiece of their effort is Camp Wellstone, an energizing and empowering weekend-long training program that teaches progressives how to integrate grassroots organizing, political campaigns, progressive public policies, and ethical leadership.

Want to be a candidate? The three-day camp covers such essentials as "the campaign plan," "dealing with the media," "the fundamentals of door-knocking," and "delivering a stump speech." Similarly, there's a three-day course on the tools and tactics needed for citizen activism and campaign management, featuring everything from coalition building to grassroots lobbying. "We teach people how to harness their own power and to take charge of the system," Blodgett said.

In only four years, they have held 105 Camp Wellstones in thirty-seven states, crisscrossing the country from Juneau to Orlando, Honolulu to Houston. With about 130 people attending each one, that's nearly 14,000 people trained in the nuts and bolts of effective political action. In addition, Wellstone Action holds special training camps

---

WALZING TO CONGRESS

Tim Walz is a salt-of-the-earth Midwesterner who simply got fed up with Bush's war and autocratic arrogance, as well as with Congress's constant kowtowing to corporate interests. So this high school teacher, football coach, and twenty-nine-year veteran of the Army National Guard from Mankato, Minnesota, decided to take a stand by running for Congress. The political pros totally dismissed him as being hopelessly out of his league. How was this novice, this complete unknown, even going to break 20 percent against the well-funded, six-term incumbent in a rural district that George W. had carried twice?

But Tim went to school. In 2005, he went through Camp Wellstone's candidate program. One of his top staffers, Leah Solo, was also a Wellstone grad, having completed the advanced campaign management school. They put together a grassroots organization, and Tim's straightforward populist message began to resonate with voters. He didn't do focus groups or play games with words. He was true to himself. He also absolutely devoured the Bush-hugging incumbent in a televised debate. To the surprise of the cognoscenti (including the National Democratic Party, which had ignored him), Walz got 53 percent of the vote, becoming one of four Camp Wellstone grads elected to Congress in 2006.

for labor organizing, students, and people trying to end domestic violence (a priority issue for Sheila). Overall, the organization has a network of 140 trainers, drawn from the ranks of top organizers.

Already, the effort is producing impressive results. Since 2004, there have been seventy-nine graduates of the Wellstone candidate schools elected in twenty states. The offices they hold are very diverse, ranging from Congressman (Keith Ellison of Minnesota, John Hall of New York, Dave Loesback of Iowa, and Tim Walz of Minnesota, all elected in 2006) to school board member, with sixty having been elected to state legislative seats.

These progressives tend to be younger, thirty of them are women, many have defeated old-line incumbents (including in primary elections), and many more are winning in suburbs and other areas once considered too conservative for progressive victories. "There's a new wave of people stepping forward to run for office," Blodgett reported. "They're authentic, rooted in their communities, and not slick career politicians afraid to take a stand or say what they really think."

With such quality candidates—backed by the skilled organizers, managers, and activists coming out of the Wellstone camps—policy changes are taking place. Look at Minnesota, where the earliest training sessions were held. In the 2004 and 2006 legislative races, twenty-two Wellstone grads were elected to the state House, thus turning control from Republican to Democratic.

Led by these energetic progressive newcomers, who're not tied to the business-as-usual crowd, the House has been making some early headway, including expanding health care to more people and passing a program to produce 25 percent of Minnesota's energy from renewable sources by 2025—one of the most ambitions programs in the country. All of this is being achieved by regular people, many of whom never considered running for office and most of whom could not have gotten there without the knowledge and the confidence building that come from training.

Even more significant than the candidates' getting elected are the democratic networks that are being developed. People are learning that there's no fairy dust in politics. It's just old-fashioned community organizing.

Lorraine Bieber, a 2006 graduate of Camp Wellstone, is a thirty-four-year-old activist from Columbus, Ohio, where she's been organizing a group that political pros disregarded as clueless and unconcerned—"youth." But it's nonsense that young people are unconcerned (you think little matters like war, wages, health care, and education aren't on their minds?). Unfortunately, they're largely unconnected, unappealed to, and unorganized. So Bieber has reached out to her young peers in the area through an innovative, youth-focused group with a spunky name: League of Pissed Off Voters.

> A bumper sticker guaranteed to terrify any political establishment, national, state, or local: "We're Pissed Off and We Vote!"

Again, no magic was involved in the effort. The goal was to get young people to contact one another and create their own politics that was fun, engaging, and relevant. Organizing around such key social issues as a ballot measure to hike Ohio's minimum wage, Lorraine targeted ten local areas that had high concentrations of young people. She set up a "Rep Your Block" program in which politically active young volunteers from the neighborhood would hold community functions, throw parties, and go door-to-door to build personal relationships among the area's young residents. The residents themselves felt involved, became invested in the political results, and became their own leaders in a bottom-up political process.

Wellstone Action takes us back to the basics of democracy: ordinary folks getting together and getting organized to be self-governing. This not only means that We the People can choose our own representatives, but that we can also keep them honest by having the ongoing ability to pull them down if they disappoint us. It puts grassroots people—not the candidates—in charge of the agenda, and allows us to put some progress back in "progressive."

CHAPTER 12

Build It!

A s my momma used to say, "You can put a sack of flour in the oven, but it won't come out biscuits."

(*Disclosure*: Actually, Lillie Mabel Hightower never said any such thing. While she's from the country, she's not much given to country sayings. But she is a lifelong biscuit maker, and she'd certainly agree with the observation.)

Good biscuits seem simple, but they don't just happen. They take care, preparation, and a practiced hand. You've got to measure, sift, mix, stir, knead, roll, and cut—all before exposing the biscuits to the heat. And you can't be afraid to get your hands sticky in the process.

It's the same with democracy.

(Good gravy, Marge, did they just compare our precious democracy to a biscuit?!)

We did. Precious democracy is not something you find, but something you make. It requires building and nurturing the grassroots base. Democracy builders are our experienced hands. They are the individuals, the groups, and the institutions that retain the collective knowledge, teach the techniques, share the tools, and spread a progressive movement.

This is politics with a long vision. It's not focused on who's running for office right now, but on creating a political infrastructure to support progressive issues and goals over the long haul. These democracy builders are community organizers, independent media people, Internet designers, grassroots fund-raisers, public interest researchers, coalition builders, educators, motivators, community lawyers, artists, festival organizers, and so many others. Maybe you?

For those who don't want to run for office or put their energies behind particular candidates, this is a place to do essential and satisfying political work. It's also a home for anyone who wants to break the grip of corporate politics, for the very nature of this pro-democracy work is antiestablishment.

Meet some people who are doing it.

THE POWER OF AN ACORN

In 1820, Felix Walker was a U.S. Congress critter from Buncombe County, North Carolina. Like many pols throughout history, Walker was a droner—a dull fellow intent on expressing his dullness on every topic and at great length. Whatever subject came up for debate on any given day, he insisted that his constituents back home would want his voice heard, and he then launched into a long and wearisome discourse that he called "a speech for Buncombe." Exasperated colleagues began to refer to his endless prattling as "just so much buncombe," a term that has been passed down to us as "bunkum," or, more pointedly, "bunk"—a synonym for meaningless political claptrap.

That's what folks of modest and low incomes are used to getting from the political system. There are liberals who want to "give'" certain benefits to the less fortunate—benefits that ultimately aren't delivered or fall way short of the need or end up being taken away. Then there are conservatives who simply want to berate lower-income people for a lack of initiative and for having bad morals. The one thing neither group wants to see is for these millions of people to become empowered, because then they would confront both the corporate and the political order (excuse the redundancy there) to achieve their own sense of justice.

It was an abundance of liberal-conservative bunkum that back in 1970 allowed a group named ACORN to sprout—a grassroots, populist effort to organize low-wage communities so they would have the power to win changes through direct action, negotiation, legislation, and voter participation.

It began when George Wiley, the smart, charismatic founder of the National Welfare Rights Organization, realized in the late 1960s that very-low-income people were destined to remain a small minority with limited power in the American system unless they could forge an alliance with those living a rung or two higher on the economic ladder—people who were also being knocked down by the Powers That Be. To give this broader strategy a try, Wiley dispatched a young, savvy, tireless, and talented organizer, Wade Rathke, to Little Rock, Arkansas.

All Rathke had to do was unite such disparate constituencies as black welfare mothers and low-income Southern whites in a state that was deeply divided racially. At the time, this seemed as impossible as trying to herd cats. However, *anyone who says you can't herd cats never tried a can opener.*

Rathke's can opener was the notion of the common interest. As Jesse Jackson would put it a decade or so later, "We might not all have come over in the same boat, but we're in the same boat now." That's a powerful, uniting political realization, and Rathke put it to work to form the Arkansas Community Organizations for Reform Now: ACORN.

This was not a mere organization but a *movement* that would grow, adapt, branch out, and flourish. Over the years, it would unite races, join neighborhoods, and link the dreams of the have-nots and the have-littles.

Thirty-seven years after its Arkansas start, ACORN (renamed the Association of Community Organizations for Reform Now) has become America's largest neighborhood-based group fighting for economic justice. It has some 350,000 members in 110 cities in 39 states, plus new organizing efforts in Argentina, Canada, Mexico, and Peru.

ACORN's organizing model has been to take on the local concerns of a particular community (utility bills, bank redlining, air and water pollution, the lack of affordable housing, poverty wages, lead paint poisoning, etc.) and link them to coordinated national actions that target those responsible: major corporations, bank-holding companies, government agencies, politicians, and other highly visible agents of established power.

The great strength of ACORN is that it gives members a chance to assert their collective power by taking action on issues that their own communities define. The heart of its work is old-fashioned, face-to-face, door-to-door organizing.

Working with a start-up committee of local residents recruited by ACORN, organizers systematically walk the neighborhood, holding casual front-porch conversations in which people

> "Almost without fail, our members say that the reason they joined ACORN is that 'no one ever came to my door and asked for *my* opinion before.'"
>
> —Maude Hurd, ACORN national president

are asked what concerns them, what makes them angry, what their hopes are. Then there's a neighborhood-wide meeting, where residents form a chapter, elect their own officers, and choose a set of issues to push. Within days, the new chapter does something about one of the items on its agenda, giving members their first taste of the fun of collective action.

What it amounts to is civic education. Very few members have ever been active in community decision making, so they learn how to work together, how to operate in the public sphere, and how to see themselves as political players with the actual *power* to get things done. As each new chapter develops and achieves some local victories, members begin to see the broader agenda of economic justice, to make links with people they never would have met without ACORN, and to connect their neighborhood needs with those of other cities, states . . . and the nation.

Not only has ACORN become a master of practicing the grassroots gospel of Organize-Strategize-Mobilize, but it also does this with a dash of sass that energizes its own people, discombobulates the stuffed shirts of the power structure, attracts widespread public attention to its issues . . . and gets results. Here's a sampling:

- Missouri senator Jim Talent had been part of a GOP cabal to keep killing congressional legislation to raise our nation's paltry minimum wage of $5.15 an hour. So, in 2006, St. Louis ACORN members decided to knock on Talent's office door—and knock on his thick head. They showed up toting a large box of old shoes. Each pair of footwear was labeled with one of America's least-desirable minimum-wage jobs. The members challenged their senator to walk a day in each set of shoes, doing the jobs of people whose wages he was holding beneath the poverty level. No go, of course. Talent's staff said that the honorable lawmaker was "unavailable" to talk with them, much less walk in non-Gucci shoes. ACORN, however, did lots of its own walking, sending members door-to-door to collect signatures to put a state minimum-wage hike on the November ballot and to register tens of thousands of new Missouri voters. They also informed voters of the senator's refusal even to talk with them about minimum wage. On Election Day, the ACORN initiative won . . . and Talent did not. His low-wage stance was not the only reason for the senator's defeat, but it was an energizing issue for many of the thousands of voters organized by ACORN, and they provided the margin in a race that he lost by only forty-eight thousand votes.

- A utility company in Gary, Indiana, had notoriously high rates and a nasty habit of pulling the plug on financially strapped folks who fell behind on their winter heating bills. Individually, low-income customers had no power to stop the quick shutoffs. But, organized into an ACORN chapter, they learned how to confront the company and make their collective voice heard. Accompanied by the media, about a dozen local ACORNers went to the utility's busy payment center in 2006, got in line, and politely waited to pay their bills . . . *in pennies*. The first one to reach the teller dumped thousands of the one-cent coins on the counter to cover her bill (literally to the penny). The wide-eyed teller looked down the line to see the other customers wearing ACORN's signature red T-shirts and toting Hefty bags of pennies. A call was made, a corporate officer came scurrying out, and a meeting was quickly arranged for ACORN to speak to the utility's president about a moratorium on shutoffs. The meeting resulted in a reduction in utility bills for some customers, and ACORN continues to negotiate and organize to achieve full reform of the utility's customer practices.

- An ACORN chapter in Toronto held a highly publicized cockroach derby in which low-income renters raced bugs they brought from their apartment buildings. The action won repairs from the shamed landlord.

- To make progress in a lengthy nationwide loan-sharking battle against the Household Finance Corporation (HFC), delegates to ACORN's 2002 national convention in Chicago thoroughly embarrassed the lender's top executives and board members. Some two thousand ACORN members spread out to upscale enclaves where the corporate honchos live, knocking on the doors of neighbors and distributing WANTED posters that featured the bigwigs and said "Wanted for Predatory Lending." This action helped close the deal on a large multistate settlement between ACORN and the HFC.

- In Minnesota, an ACORN member moved out of an apartment after a rat bit her baby. The property owners said that by leaving she had broken her lease, and they sent the account to a collection agency to force her to pay the remainder of the rent due under the lease. The local ACORN chapter responded en masse, going to the landlord's office wearing rat noses. When a startled company official tried to turn them away saying that they couldn't come barging in without an appointment, one of the members didn't miss a beat, retorting, "That rat didn't have an appointment when it bit her baby." The owners agreed to cancel the woman's lease and clear her credit report.

> "Ordinary citizens step up to do ACORN work. Once you get involved, you will never be satisfied with grumbling again. After getting organized and making change happen, you can never go back to doing nothing."
>
> —Toni McElroy, chair, Texas ACORN

Well into their fourth decade of agitating and organizing, ACORN's members have become a formidable force for producing progressive change in low-income neighborhoods, and ACORN itself is now an American institution. It is not merely scrappy; it is strong and capable of sustaining long-term community development and grassroots political action. The annual budget of the nationwide ACORN network is nearly $37 million, which comes from members' dues ($10 a month or less), services it provides, and occasional grants. With special training centers for organizers, its own housing development corporation, a separate research arm, two radio stations, and more than a hundred offices from coast to coast, ACORN can go toe-to-toe with the corporate and political powers that usually consider low-income working folks easy to run over.

A LIVING WAGE

It's interesting that our society commonly uses the expression "to wage war," for the matter of wages has most certainly been at the center of many wars (bloody and otherwise) in our country's history. Just look at how corporate interests and their obedient troops in Congress constantly engage in class war to hold down the wages of America's workers.)

One deplorable example was the stingy, decade-long refusal to raise the minimum wage above $5.15 an hour. That's $10,500 a year *gross* (in both meanings of that word) for full-time work. Under $200 a week, this left hardworking people thousands of dollars below the poverty line. It's impossible to stretch that to cover even the basics of living: rent, utilities, groceries, transportation, clothing, and medicines.

Yet, even when the new Democratic Congress finally raised the minimum wage in 2007, the initial hike was only 70 cents an hour—still abject poverty. After two years, the minimum wage is to rise to $7.25 an hour. That's better, but by then the real value of this wage will have deflated to about $6.42 an hour—roughly $13,000 a year—which will still leave full-time workers mired in poverty.

Think of what that says about our society, which happens to be the wealthiest in the history of the world. The minimum wage is the ethical floor that we choose to set, and it's a moral abomination that our so-called leaders say it's okay to reward America's vaunted work ethic with poverty.

Meanwhile, since 1997, guess how many times the chuckle-heads in Congress have raised their own pay? Bingo, if you said eight! Lawmakers now take $165,200 each in annual pay. (*Warning: the following comment could cause some readers to lose their lunch.*) Asked a few years ago about these self-propelled pay hikes, then majority leader Tom DeLay snapped, "I challenge anyone to live on my salary."

Rather than wait for Congress to be struck by a random bolt of sanity, ACORN became the leader of a phenomenal grassroots economic movement to win raises for millions of low-paid workers. Its members (again, people of limited incomes who have traditionally had no clout in economic and political decisions) have led successful campaigns in fifteen cities and led efforts in eight states to raise the minimum wage above the ignoble federal level.

The central concept behind these campaigns is called the "living wage." What's a living wage? Simple: *It's a wage a family can live on without having to go Dumpster diving once a week.* More than a minimum, a living wage is a measure of social decency, set at least high enough to ensure that an American working family does not reside in poverty.

In addition to the campaigns that ACORN has directly run, it has been a key member of coalitions that have passed living wage laws (mostly through ballot initiatives) in 140 cities and passed hikes in dozens of states. While the establishment media have largely ignored it, this is a widespread and remarkably successful movement, delivering a significant economic (and spiritual) lift for low-income workers all across the country—*and the people themselves are causing the change.*

Like churches and unions that are also integral to the success of the living wage coalition, ACORN has the institutional staying power to keep pushing. In 1998, it created the Living Wage Resource Center within its organization to provide training, research, campaign materials, strategy, and direct assistance to local organizers and coalitions that are trying to increase minimum pay. The center has become a major force in spreading the success of the living wage movement and also in strengthening the grassroots groups that form it.

William Kyser and the ACORN chapter in his Albuquerque neighborhood show the importance of this staying power. Kyser's family joined in 2004, and the next year, William found himself in the thick of the chapter's effort to raise the city's minimum wage to $7.50 an hour. By then, he had become the host of ACORN's TV talk show

---

ACORN 71, KERRY 47

In 2004, ACORN and allies collected nearly a million signatures from fed-up Floridian voters to put a modest $1 increase in the state minimum wage on the ballot. As expected, Governor Jeb Bush and Florida's business establishment went all out to kill it. What was not expected was that John Kerry, then the Democratic presidential nominee, would be such a wuss.

The geniuses advising Kerry shooed him away from endorsing the wage initiative, insisting that Florida was too conservative to pass it and that he should not taint himself with an unpopular reform.

Yet on election night, ACORN members were the ones celebrating. *Their initiative passed with 71 percent of the vote—carrying every county.* Meanwhile, things were less cheerful over at Kerry headquarters. The guy who was too skittish to touch the minimum-wage increase got only 47 percent of the vote.

on the local public access channel, and he put it to work, bringing economists, city council members, and minimum-wage workers from such outfits as McDonald's to inform and energize the community.

"I'm not Merv Griffin," William said, "but I like talking to people." He also faced off twice in debates with the Albuquerque chamber of commerce CEO, and the whole Kyser family helped ACORN gather thirty-three thousand signatures to get the wage increase on the ballot. It was a tremendous organizing effort, but the business interests (no surprise) dumped a truckload of cash into the fight, and the initiative was narrowly defeated.

In too many progressive battles, that would have been the end. Volunteers would be discouraged, money would dry up, and the coalition would disperse. With ACORN, however, a loss can be seen as a learning experience and a building block for the next step. "We've got people talking about the wage increase now," William said buoyantly, just after the 2005 vote. "We've learned a lot. I think we know now how to pass it." And they did. ACORN came back in 2006 to win in Albuquerque, and in 2007 it got New Mexico's legislature to extend the pay raise statewide.

This kind of success is the direct result of organizing and nurturing genuine grassroots political power. In 2006, ACORN members led coalition efforts to win minimum-wage hikes in Arizona (66 percent voted yes), Colorado (53 percent yes), Missouri (76 percent yes), and Ohio (56 percent yes). In these states, ACORN registered more than two hundred thousand new voters in low-income neighborhoods—and then it stuck with these and other voters through the election, visiting them door-to-door multiple times, involving them personally, and making them feel crucial to the election outcomes (which, of course, they were).

One of the most effective components of ACORN's organizing structure is its PAL program. PALs are Precinct Action Leaders who are recruited from the neighborhoods and trained to build strong networks among their neighbors for civic participation. Each of the volunteer PALs creates and services a list of about a hundred friends, family members, and other residents in his or her immediate community. The PALs are responsible for staying in touch with each voter on their list to make sure that the voters are registered, informed, and ready to vote.

The election, however, is just the start, for the PAL process builds ongoing political relationships, generating neighborhood power that lasts beyond any single election cycle. The community learns that its votes can produce changes that it cares about, so staying engaged actually matters. "Neighborhoods with a higher voter turnout get more respect and more resources from politicians. That's just a fact," noted John Shields, an ACORN PAL in Missouri.

This is a fact that affluent neighborhoods have long known—and have tried to keep their little secret. But the secret is out. People all across the country are learning that they really do have the power to rule—if they get themselves organized. The assertion of democratic strength in ACORN neighborhoods is a textbook example of what it means to be self-governing . . . and how satisfying the results can be.

CHAPTER 13

Granny Power

There's an old cliché that smug right-wingers like to spout:

If you're not a liberal at twenty, you have no heart.

But if you're not a conservative at forty, you have no brain.

DeMarco and I, however, offer a third phase in life:

If you're not a radical at sixty, you haven't paid attention.

Lest you think that our message (*Have you forgotten it already?! Executive summary*: Defy the corporate order/Live your values) is meant only for youngsters just starting out or for midlife people yearning to make a break for something more meaningful, you old-sters should know that you (which, by the way, includes us) are in a special position to step out, question authority, and stand up for progressive values. Several factors are in your favor.

1. You're old. You've lived a long time, you know how the system works, and you can't be fooled by the establishment's false promises—you have knowledge and experience to share.

2. You're old. You have some credibility and a smidgen of social respect, both of which come with age. Use them to confront the ruling powers.

3. You're old. What have you got to lose? Lawn bowling, bridge, and golf are fine, but what difference do they make? Let's be honest: the clock is ticking. If you haven't broken loose yet, it's time. You can still make a difference.

4. You're old. With all the aches and assorted ailments that age brings, you're already paying the price of your years—so you deserve some fun!

One exemplary group that's doing all of this is the Granny Peace Brigade. These eighteen New York ladies (ranging from sixty to ninety-one years of age) made a bold statement against the Iraq war in October 2005.

Although they had not known one another before coming together through peace groups that were organizing in the city, they were united in anger at Bush's disastrous misadventure in Iraq, and they shared a determination to do something about it. One thing they had in common was the status of "family elder."

In an inspired action that was both whimsical and serious, the eighteen arrived en masse—some with canes and walkers—at a military recruitment center in Times Square. They came to volunteer to be sent to Iraq in place of the young people who would otherwise have to go. "Kill us, not them," was their plea—a grandmotherly keening to focus public attention on the deadly price of George W.'s lying arrogance. "We insist we enlist," they chanted as they approached the center.

Startled recruiters responded by hurriedly locking the door and telling them to go away. Ha! Not a chance the army could run off this bunch. The women simply sat down, right in front of the center's door. Flabbergasted, the U.S. military then called the cops on the grannies.

With TV cameras and scribes capturing the moment, NYPD officers young enough to be their grandchildren arrested the eighteen women. They were handcuffed (far more gently than others might expect to be treated), loaded into police vans, and hauled off to jail, where they were booked and charged with blocking a public entrance and refusing to move.

Manhattan's longtime district attorney Robert Morgenthau (at eighty-six, no spring chicken himself) didn't need the PR headache of putting a covey of grandmothers on trial. So he proposed a plea deal that would dismiss their charges in six months, provided the ladies stayed out of "trouble."

Ha, again! The grannies were on a mission, and every one of them wanted her day in court to say her piece. As Molly Klopot, eighty-seven, put it: "We are at a very important point in the history of our country. It is our responsibility as patriots not to be silent." Vinnie Burrows Harrison (don't ask her age) added, "You have to stand up for something or you mean nothing."

> "Grandmas, let's unite while we are still upright."
>
> —A Peace Brigade chant

Six months after the sit-in, a six-day trial began. The prosecution asserted that this was nothing but a disorderly conduct case, but the grannies' defense lawyers contended that it was about the right of all Americans to protest the *dishonorable* conduct of their government.

The ladies hung tough as the prosecutors probed their actions. Judy Lear, sixty-two, was asked, "Isn't it true you were blocking the entrance?" Ms. Lear replied that she would have gladly moved aside if anyone had wanted to go through: "I'm a very polite person."

The prosecution tried mocking them as mere publicity seekers. Diane Dreyfus, sixty, was asked whether she seriously could have thought that she would be allowed to enlist. "I wasn't sure," she said. "I do have a skill set." "Yes, yes, but you wouldn't really have been willing to go to war," the prosecution countered. "Yes, I was totally prepared," responded Ms. Dreyfus. "I had just recently gotten divorced. I was ready."

After closing arguments in this non–jury trial, the judge found that the Granny Peace Brigade had not blocked anyone from entering the recruitment center and, therefore, the women had been wrongly arrested. "The defendants are all discharged," he said, with a bang of the gavel. Outside the courthouse, the joyful group burst into cheers when their lead lawyer said to them, "The decision today says the First Amendment protects you to protest peacefully. So—go do it!" And they've continued to do just that.

Columnist Ellen Goodman later asked some of the grannies why they were protesting when their children and grandchildren were not. "They're busy; we're all retired," said Joan Wile, seventy-four. Molly Klopot added, "We helped the world get in the shape it's in. We have some responsibility here." All of them agreed with another truly liberating notion: "We've reached a wonderful stage in life called 'nothing left to lose.'"

Then there are the Raging Grannies, a musical protest troupe with chapters (they call them "granny gaggles") all across the country. They wear flamboyant, flowery hats, dress in classic granny attire, and sing old tunes that they've reworked with satirical antiwar lyrics. They're a hoot! We first saw them at a fair in Maine, where they delivered a serious message sweetened with their colorful hats, humor, and a dance routine. They were quite good, which they attributed to the fact that they practiced. Naturally—we knew that. They seemed to be having as much fun as the crowd was.

Meanwhile, clear across the country on the Berkeley campus of the University of California, three women added their maturity to a conservation protest by doing something they probably hadn't done since girlhood: they climbed a tree.

In January 2007, the Live Oak Three—Shirley Dean, seventy-one; Betty Olds, eighty-six; and Sylvia McLaughlin, ninety—hoisted themselves up a ladder onto a makeshift platform nestled in a coastal live oak. The tree is part of a small grove of about fifty beautiful oaks,

Even in death, you can take a parting shot. When Ted Heller passed away in 2005 at the age of eighty-eight, his obituary in the *Chicago Tribune* contained an unusual request: "In lieu of flowers, please send acerbic letters to Republicans."

some said to be more than two hundred years old (although the one that the three climbed was a mere ninety, just like Sylvia). The purpose of the climb was to rally public opposition to the university's plan to cut down most of the grove. It seems that this small urban forest had very selfishly chosen to grow up on a spot that the University of California now claimed it needed for a $125 million athletic training center and parking garage.

A "save the oaks" group (which included environmentalists, students, neighborhood associations, and others) had been protesting the university's proposal for several weeks with an ongoing "tree-sit," and our three ladies were adding their gray eminence to the cause. Using a bullhorn to address reporters and a crowd that had gathered, Shirley brought cheers when she declared, "We have 250 years of experience between us. Nobody's going to cut us down, and no one's going to cut down these trees!"

Taking a stand for the trees was the easy part for Shirley. Actually being so high above the ground was the hard part. She spent the entire time clutching a branch, confessing, "I'm scared to death of heights." But obviously not scared of mighty university regents and their scowling lawyers.

Amazingly, not even Sylvia was the oldest activist at the event. That honor went to Margaret Emmington, who was 102 at the time! While she didn't climb the ladder, she had trekked up the hillside in her hat, dress, and pumps to take her stand. "I feel it's vital for the university to preserve its forest," she avouched.

The coalition won a victory a week later when a superior court judge granted an injunction that spared the trees from the university's saws—at least temporarily. The "save the oaks" tree-sitters, however, are not letting their guard down, vowing to stay in the branches until the University of California agrees to a permanent plan that will protect the grove. And if school officials try to pull a fast one, the seventy-, eighty-, and ninety-somethings are ready to climb again.

CHAPTER 14

The Politics of Fun

Lewis Grizzard, the late humorist, was a very helpful interpreter of Southern culture. For example, he once explained the important difference between someone being naked . . . and nekkid:

> "Naked" means you have no clothes on.

> "Nekkid" means you have no clothes on, *and* you're up to something.

Our friend Ed Garvey is not Southern, but he's a political sprite who's constantly up to something—and it's invariably for the greater good. Plus, you can always count on it being fun.

Based in Madison, Wisconsin, Ed is a people's lawyer who relishes battling the bastards and standing up for underdogs. He's a populist scrapper, with many successful fights under his belt. He went head-to-head with the NFL owners' association and won the first union contract for pro football players. He took on Perrier Inc. and stopped this global water plunderer from grabbing the pure springwater of a small Wisconsin town. He also came just a few votes short of unseating a money-grubbing U.S. senator in the 1986 general election. There's an old Irish saying that sums up this Irishman's approach to any injustice: "Is this a private fight or can anyone join?"

In September 2001, Ed and nine other veterans of various scrapes with the forces of avarice and malice got together for a Saturday morning coffee klatch at a Perkins restaurant out in the Wisconsin Dells. Over sausage and eggs, they kicked around ideas about what they might do to cope with an ongoing problem: progressives are disorganized.

More specifically, the group had learned that whenever a corporate power descends upon an area with some particular larceny in mind, it always arrives with money, lawyers and lobbyists, a well-practiced plan of action, and at least a couple of local politicians in its back pocket. Citizens' groups, on the other hand, usually start from scratch when they rise up to oppose the latest corporate outrages. Most local groups think they're the first ones to face this sort of assault. With little connection to others who've fought similar battles, they scramble. Who owns this corporation? How do you file a freedom of information action? What's an environmental impact statement?

The Perkins 10 are folks who'd been through such fights in their communities—some battling Perrier, some Wal-Mart, some Exxon-Mobil—and they wanted to spread their hard-won knowledge of how corporate forces work. They dreamed of a statewide network of citizens who would be willing to help one another in future fights.

The group decided to hold a sizable gathering to link this loose grassroots base together. Their idea was to form a sort of citizens' strike force with the potential to leap into action when the call came and to share information so that communities didn't have to reinvent the wheel for every struggle.

Guess who said "This is a great idea, but let's make it fun"? Our boy Ed, naturally. He recalled that at the turn of the twentieth century, Wisconsin had been a hot spot for the Chautauqua movement—large gatherings to discuss the issues of the day, hear music and speakers, bring the family, camp out, eat together, play games, learn, and enjoy. Why not do something like that again?

"Let's give it a name," said one of the Perkins 10. "I know," said another, "our state's most famous hell-raiser is Fighting Bob La Follette. Let's name it for him." Thus was born the Fighting Bob Fest.

But where to hold it? Maybe a farm, a park, or a fairground. Sites were scouted, and an ideal one was found in the town of Baraboo, about fifty miles north of Madison. The original headquarters and winter home of the Ringling Brothers Circus, Baraboo offered just the right symbol, location, and spirit for a festival, and its Sauk County Fairground is the perfect site for what has become a daylong "county fair of politics and fun."

How to pay for it? This is often the question that stops good ideas in their tracks, but the only honest answer is the one the Perkins 10 gave to themselves: "Somehow, it'll work out. People will come and we'll pass the hat." The group figured that the price tag on the first Bob Fest would be ten to fifteen thousand bucks, and they agreed to chip in for the up-front costs and to cover any losses. Also—key to the event's success—the whole shebang was to be volunteer. No paid speakers, musicians, or staff, and as many donated supplies and services as possible.

So, they began. The headquarters were in Ed's law office, and his small staff served as the initial coordinators. The *Capital Times*, Madison's populist, independent daily newspaper (founded in 1917 by a La Follette devotee who wanted a paper to champion the people over corporate power), chipped in a $7,500 grant and agreed to promote the Fest. The organizers used the Internet, activist lists, and word-of-mouth to draw a crowd . . . they hoped.

On Saturday, September 7, 2002, it happened. Former senator Paul Simon of Illinois was the featured speaker. As Ed drove to Baraboo early that morning, he figured that if only fifty people showed up, he'd assure the senator that they were "the very best fifty people in Wisconsin." When the gates swung open, however, more than fifty cars were already lined up to get in, and cars kept coming. More than a thousand people attended Bob Fest I.

In 2003, there were 2,500 participants. The next year, 4,000 came, then 5,000 in 2005, 6,000 in 2006, and more than 7,000 last year. Seven thousand is at least ten times more people than show up for either a Republican or a Democratic state convention.

FIGHTING BOB

> The supreme issue, involving all others, is the encroachment of the powerful few on the rights of the many. This mighty power has come between the people and their government. . . . [It] can only be overthrown by resisting at every step, seizing upon every important occasion which offers opportunity to uncover the methods of the system.
>
> —Robert M. La Follette, 1922

Born in 1855, La Follette was elected to Congress in 1884 as a Republican. His Republicanism embraced the ideals of Lincoln, and he spent most of the 1890s forming a progressive wing of the party. This was not easy since the railroad barons, the lumber giants, and the bank cartels controlled the GOP nationally and in Wisconsin. But La Follette and others rallied the state's working families to build a political base that was capable of fighting the corporate powers, and they succeeded in electing him governor in 1900.

In the first decade of the new century, La Follette and fellow progressives in the legislature brought monumental change: a progressive income tax, unemployment compensation, bank and railroad regulations, and other pro-farmer and pro-worker laws that laid the groundwork for what would become the New Deal.

Fighting Bob went on to the U.S. Senate, where he pushed for programs to rein in runaway corporate power. Frustrated by the slow pace of progress, he finally broke with the Republicans. In 1924, he created the Progressive Party and ran as its candidate for president, drawing nearly a fourth of the votes. La Follette died in 1925, having become an inspiration for progressives all across the country who want to unshackle the people from the greed of special interests. As La Follette said of this ongoing struggle, "America is not made. It is in the making."

Why do they come? Ed said that, first, most people feel politically homeless these days, and Bob Fest is a welcoming place where they can get involved in building something significant. Second, it's not just a boring meeting—it's a festival!

Rather than having to sit in one place and be talked at, you're free to roam, and there's lots to do at this political fair for the whole family. There are two music stages, about ten food vendors (selling everything from the always-essential Wisconsin brats to roasted veggie sandwiches), about a hundred activist booths, four spaces for breakout sessions on a wide range of issues, a beer court featuring Wisconsin microbrews and a local wine (gotta keep the movement lubricated!), a bookstore and book signings, a live radio broadcast on WORT-FM, and, of course, the main speakers' stage facing the grandstand.

Among those who've been on that stage are Robert F. Kennedy Jr., Granny D, Tom Harkin, John Conyers, Amy Goodman, Lois Gibbs, Matt Gonzalez, Bernie Sanders . . . and a guy named Hightower. Even more important than the national speakers are the voices of Wisconsin's own progressive elected leaders and activists. We out-of-staters fly away the next day, but it's the ones who stay and work with the Bob-Festers over the long haul who make the biggest difference.

About 40 percent of the attendees join in the breakout sessions, choosing from a dozen topics that range from creating independent media to stopping war. There are group leaders for each one, but the emphasis is on getting the participants to talk, and focusing on solutions rather than reiterating the problems.

The festival has spun out two institutional means of keeping folks connected and spreading the word. One is FightingBob.com, an active Web site that is updated daily. It posts original articles, blogs, and other information from the network of Fest participants, and it serves as an activist alarm to alert the network about battles that need their involvement.

The second is called the People's Legislature, which is a citizen's assembly cosponsored by Fighting Bob. It enlists festivalgoers and other activist groups in the development of an agenda that all of them then carry to the capitol. In 2005, they pushed for SB1, a state ethics

"Thank you for Bob Fest. With your help, and that of other progressives I've met over the last few years, I'm starting to come back to life. This after falling asleep at the switch and letting the 1980s and '90s go by without any great effort on my part to make those years better. I'm sorry for that, but I'm back now. On a warm and sunny Saturday, I actually felt like things were going to be okay. I got angry, I got inspired, I got to laugh a lot."

—Jack Benjamin, Bob Fest participant

reform law. More than three hundred people jammed a capitol hearing room, demanding action. Two days later, the committee approved the bill, but legislative leaders refused to bring it to a floor vote. Members of the People's Legislature then picketed the capitol, and a group of them filled the House gallery, unfurling a large banner that read "Clean Up Your Act . . . Vote on Senate Bill 1." All of this got wide media coverage and drew even wider public support.

GOP leaders, however, held a closed-door session to bully their members into opposing the bill, including getting four of the SB1's Republican sponsors to kill their own legislation. "That's what the cause of reform is up against," said Mike McCabe, a leader of the grassroots coalition. "And that's why the People's Legislature needs to get even bigger and more muscular."

They got more muscular in 2006, an election year. This time, an energized brigade of citizens returned to the capitol carrying brooms and calling for "a clean sweep." Amazingly, in one of the absurd ironies you sometimes encounter in politics, the clean sweepers were stopped at the entrance and told they had to check their brooms at the door—*no brooms allowed inside the state capitol.*

Apparently, brooms could be "weapons"—and indeed they ended up being just that. The media captured the broom seizure on film, letting an appalled public see the stack of brooms being piled high at their capitol's door—an image that became a potent political weapon in the fall legislative elections. The GOP lost control of the Senate that fall, and, while no one can say that BroomGate was the cause, it sure didn't help the Republicans. In January 2007, the first thing the new legislature did was to pass SB1.

Bob Fest excites and empowers ordinary people, showing them how to get involved and be effective. The grassroots strike force that the Perkins 10 envisioned now exists, giving local progressives at least a semblance of organization and a better chance against the moneyed interests that try to bulldoze them.

The festival itself continues as a volunteer organization. Even in year one, passing the hat raised more money than was spent to produce the event, and this has been true every year since (in part because a couple of volunteers have turned out be very, very good at working the crowd, using humor and guilt to say, in essence, "It was free to get in, but not to get out—everyone needs to pony up a little something to keep Bob going"). The best news is that rank-and-file Wisconsin progressives have taken own-

> "I was there with my fiancée, my brother, and his girlfriend, and we wanted to thank you and let you know that next year we will bring more people and help spread the message that is so dear to us all."
>
> —Tyler Schueffner, Bob Fest participant

ership, so they're eager to contribute, volunteer, and become the leaders. Bob Fest shows that folks are hungry for political involvement that . . . well, that involves them.

At the last Fighting Bob Fest, people from eighteen different states attended. Many of them were interested in starting something like it where they live. Ed reminded us that there's no rule book for taking back political power. "When we decided six years ago to try it with a festival, we didn't know what we were doing or whether it would work. But you've got to start somewhere. *The main thing is to start.*"

In our view, there ought to be a Bob Fest in every state, for it's a great way to put the party back in politics. And, as Ed said, "If you can't have fun, why do it?"

Connections for Part Two

Politics comes in all sizes. Do you want to spend a little time or a lot? Will you focus locally or globally? Do you simply want your voice to be heard a bit more clearly or will you go all out by running for office? Whether you want to volunteer occasionally or work full-time at building the progressive movement, there's room for you to be more involved in public affairs. Here are some grassroots groups that will welcome, inform, involve, and assist you.

We've written about some of them in this section, and the others are activist organizations that also provide materials, contacts, networking, training, and organizing.

Oregon Bus Project
333 SE 2nd Avenue
Portland, OR 97214
Phone: (503) 233-3018
E-mail: info@busproject.org
Web Site: www.busproject.org

Public Campaign
1320 19th Street, NW, Suite M-1
Washington, DC 20036
Phone: (202) 293-0222
E-mail: info@publicampaign.org
Web Site: www.publicampaign.org

Maine Clean Elections
P.O. Box 18187
Portland, ME 04112
Phone: (207) 664-0696
E-mail: info@maineclean
    elections.org
Web Site: www.maineclean
    elections.org

Clean Elections Institute
2702 N. 3rd Street, Suite 4010
Phoenix, AZ 85004
Phone: (602) 840-6633

Web Site: www.azclean.org

North Carolina Voters for Clean Elections
P.O. Box 10402
Raleigh, NC 27605
Phone: (919) 521-4121
E-mail: ncvce.coalition@gmail .com
Web Site: www.ncvce.org

Democracy North Carolina
1821 Green Street
Durham, NC 27705
Phone: (919) 286-6000
E-mail: info@democracy-nc.org
Web Site: wwwdemocracy-nn.org

Institute for Southern Studies
P.O. Box 531
Durham, NC 27702
Phone: (919) 419-8311
Web Site: www.southernstudies .org

Doris "Granny D" Haddock
P.O. Box 492
Dublin, NH 03444
Web Site: www.grannyd.com

National Center for Science Education
420 40th Street, Suite 2
Oakland, CA 94609-2509
Phone: (510) 601-7203
E-mail: ncseoffice@ncseweb .org
Web Site: www.natcenscied.org

Wellstone Action
821 Raymond Avenue, Suite 260
St. Paul, MN 55144
Phone: (651) 645-3939
Web Site: www.wellstone.org

Representative Tim Walz, District Office
227 E. Main Street, Suite 220
Mankato, MN 56001
Phone: (507) 388-2149
Web Site: http://walz.house .gov

League of Pissed Off Voters
(now called the League of Young Voters)
45 Main Street, Suite 628
Brooklyn, NY 11201
Phone: (718) 305-4245
Web Site: www.theleague.com

ACORN (Association of Community Organizations for Reform Now)
National & Legislative Office
739 8th Street, SE
Washington, DC 20003
Toll-free: (877) 55ACORN
E-mail: natacorndc@acorn.org
Web Site: www.acorn.org

Living Wage Resource Center
739 8th Street, SE
Washington, DC 20003
Phone: (202) 547-2500
Web Site: www.livingwagecam paign.org

Granny Peace Brigade
c/o WILPF
339 Lafayette Street
New York, NY 10012
Phone: (212) 533-2125
E-mail: grannypeacebrigade@ earthink.net
Web Site: www.grannypeace brigade.org

Raging Grannies
Web Site: www.raginggrannies
.com

Save the Oaks Coalition
Berkeley, CA
Web Site: www.saveoaks.org

Fighting Bob Fest
Ed Garvey
P.O. Box 2131
Madison, WI 53701
Phone: (608) 256-1003
E-mail: comments@fightingbob
.com
Web Site: www.fightingbob.com

The People's Legislature
c/o Wisconsin Democracy
Campaign
201 North Basset Street, Suite 215
Madison, WI 53703
Phone: (608) 225-4260
Web Site: www.peopleslegislature
.org

Connect with these groups, too.

Center for Responsive Politics
1101 14th Street, NW, Suite 1030
Washington, DC 20005-5635
Phone: (202) 857-0044
E-mail: info@crp.org
Web Site: www.opensecrets.org
This site tracks who gives the big bucks to whom in presidential and congressional elections, as well as what the donors receive in return. Its online database, available to the public, is considered the most authoritative source on campaign funding.

Common Cause
1133 19th Street, NW, 9th Floor
Washington, DC 20036
Phone: (202) 833-1200
E-mail: grassroots@common
cause.org
Web Site: www.commoncause
.org
Its three hundred thousand members and thirty-six state chapters constitute an effective citizens' lobby, focusing on public financing of elections and a broad assortment of good-government issues. It works not only at the national level, but also on state and local reforms.

Democracy for America
P.O. Box 1717
Burlington, VT 05402
Phone: (802) 651-3200
Web Site: www.democracyfor
america.com
Inspired by Howard Dean's 2004 campaign, which brought thousands of new people into Democratic politics, DFA continues to expand, organize, and mobilize that energetic base into a progressive movement for grassroots-led democracy. It holds about twenty training academies a year, focusing especially on the "red" states that the Democratic establishment ignores.

Drinking Liberally
425 W. 45th Street, Suite 3FE
New York, NY 10036
Web Site: drinkingliberally.org
Why not put the party back in politics? Launched in 2004 in New

York City, this is now a nationwide network of informal, inclusive local groups of progressives who gather regularly at their favored taverns to talk politics, swap jokes, learn, vent, scheme, enjoy . . . and, of course, drink. There are now 209 chapters in 44 states. Join one . . . or start your own—they'll tell you how. There's also a Laughing Liberally comedy tour and a Screening Liberally film series.

League of Conservation Voters
1920 L Street, NW, Suite 800
Washington, DC 20036
Phone: (202) 785-8683
Web Site: www.lcv.org

With thousands of volunteers and a network of thirty-five state leagues, they can plug you into effective environmental politics. The league publishes a National Environmental Scorecard to reveal the voting records of every member of Congress.

League of Rural Voters
P.O. Box 80259
Minneapolis, MN 55408
Phone: (612) 879-7578
E-mail: info@leagueofruralvoters
    .org
Web Site: www.leagueofrural
    voters.org

With rural issues usually ignored in national politics, this outfit is strengthening the voice of rural folks by providing online advocacy tools, an action alert network, issue papers, a newsletter, and other types of assistance to help citizens hold politicians accountable.

MoveOn
Web Site: www.moveon.org

With some three million members, this Internet organizer is able to inform and mobilize rank-and-file progressives to unify their voices and have a powerful impact on major issues and elections. It is a democratic, interactive Web organization that bypasses the money interests, the media filters, and the power brokers.

Progressive Majority
1825 K Street, NW, Suite 450
Washington, DC 20006
Phone: (202) 408-8603
Web Site: www.progressivemajority
    .org

Now working with activists in twenty-four battleground states, these skilled organizers are recruiting and training local progressives to win office . . . then move up. This "farm team" approach is proving very effective; they've already elected more than two hundred quality candidates to state and local offices, bringing new talent and excitement into progressive politics.

Public Citizen
1600 20th Street, NW
Washington, DC 20009
Phone: (202) 588-1000
Web Site: www.citizen.org

One of the first public interest institutions (founded in 1971), it has ten thousand members across the country. It is a reliable source of information on a wide array of public policy issues, an effective grassroots organizer on such fights as global trade, a feisty congressional watchdog, and a preeminent battler for the public interest in legal cases.

Public Interest Research Groups (PIRG)

218 D Street, SE
Washington, DC 20003
Phone: (202) 546-9707
Web Site: www.uspirg.org

A scrappy, grassroots network that organizes local people around a broad range of issues, fights legislative battles, conducts investigative reports, supports (or opposes) ballot initiatives, and files lawsuits. It has some four hundred organizers and policy advocates, chapters in forty-seven states, and student PIRGs on nearly a hundred campuses.

True Majority

191 Bank Street, Third Floor
Burlington, VT 05401
Phone: (802) 860-6858
Web Site: www.truemajority.org

True Majority is both an online and an on-the-ground activist group, founded by the puckish Ben Cohen, of Ben & Jerry's ice cream fame. From poverty to the bloated Pentagon budget, True Majority enlists the grassroots in pointed, effective, and fun political activism.

PART THREE

"*The significant problems we have cannot be solved at the same level of thinking with which we created them.*"

—Albert Einstein

CHAPTER 15

Take Charge!

Sometimes, it's the small things in life that leave me stumped. Things like:

- Glue. Why doesn't it stick to the inside of the bottle?
- When Noah brought two of every species aboard the Ark, where did he put the termites?
- The guy who invented bagpipes—what was he really trying to do?

By nature, we are a questioning species. After "Mommy" and "Daddy," the first word shaped by our baby brains is "Why?" Indeed, many a toddler has driven parents bonkers with the incessant, high-pitched repetition of this query.

But as we get older, "Why?" becomes a radical question when directed to the actions of the Powers That Be—which is why most established institutions go out of their way to teach us, from school age forward, that ours is not to reason why. Accept things as they are, we are instructed, and just keep repeating to yourself:

It's for my own good.

It's in the national interest.

It's the natural order of things.

It's the magic of the marketplace.

The experts know best.

This mantra is foisted on us not only in the fields of business and politics, but also in the very conduct of our lives. The reigning ethos of America's corporate culture—its official religion, really—is consumerism. Kids, for example, no longer just go out and play. They plug in to their electronic gizmos, buy expensive brand-name outfits, get booked for playdates, and learn from an early age that life's reward is buying stuff.

Consumerism is not a "life," it's a substitute for life. To elevate it to the level of a predominant social goal demeans the human spirit, restricts our potential, distorts our society, and endangers our world. It's essential (and uplifting) that more and more people these days are questioning this superficial ethos, looking for something deeper, and, in essence, asking, "What is life?"

After all, we Americans are not condemned to be passive recipients of whatever is doled out to us. We're a stronger people than that, possessing both the individual fortitude and the collective rebelliousness to make big changes in the economic and social terms of how we live. It's not the metaphysical that people are exploring, but the practicalities and the personal aspects of living in a way that can be at once more satisfying and more suited to our moral beliefs than what the shallow consumer system dictates.

The basic question is this:

> Will we let greedheaded profiteers determine the boundaries of our lives? Or will we take charge, blazing new paths for ourselves and our country?

It's in our character to question authority. After all, that's how America came to be. And, periodically, We the People have had to make a hard assessment of where we were headed as a society . . . and make important corrections to the course. Over generations, it has been this questioning instinct of grassroots people that has sparked a continuum of progressive changes. Corrections such as ending slavery have been huge moral shifts. Such others as public education have profoundly altered the way we live, more closely reflecting our egalitarian values.

Every important change began with commonsense people having doubts about the status quo and asking questions aloud, which emboldened others to say, "You know, I was wondering about that same thing." When enough people spoke up, a social awakening spread, and multitudes of people started to take action individually and in groups. At this point, the people became a movement . . . and change began to happen.

THE UPCHUCK REBELLION

This is not a phenomenon you find only in history books but is a living, integral part of our society. In fact, right now, we're in the midst of a dramatic revolt over something that touches each of our lives every day in the most basic way: dinner.

During the last fifty years, control over America's food policies quietly shifted from farmers and consumers to corporate executives, shortsighted bureaucrats, and economists. These are people who could not run a watermelon stand if we gave them the melons and had the highway patrol flag down customers for them. Yet they took charge of the decisions that direct everything from how food is grown and processed to what our children eat in school.

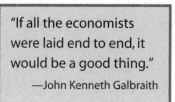

"If all the economists were laid end to end, it would be a good thing."

—John Kenneth Galbraith

They were not good deciders, because their interests are not ours. Agricorps don't see food as a juicy, luscious, nutritious product of nature but as a profit center to be conglomeratized, industrialized, and globalized. We're not talking about the making of some computer gadget here, but about our dinner! The natural state of food production is that it's small-scale, agrarian, and local. This is because plants and animals are living creatures. Economies of scale are achieved at a surprisingly small level, with both productivity and quality being enhanced by the ability of farmers and artisans to be personally involved with their crops and livestock

But the agribusiness powers perverted agriculture production from the high art and science of cooperating with nature into a high-cost, high-tech process of overwhelming nature.

To say that they take shortcuts with food in their mad dash for profits understates reality. Let's be blunt: they *torture* food. They apply massive doses of pesticides and artificial fertilizers to these living organisms. They inject animals with antibiotics and sex hormones. They turn lab technicians loose to alter the very DNA of organisms, manufacturing mutant "Frankenfoods." They force grass-eating cows to become carnivores and even cannibals. They blast fruits and veggies with ripening gas and zap them with radiation. They dose the finished foodstuffs with assorted sugars, artificial flavorings, trans fats, and chemical preservatives. What we're left with is "food" that has lost all connection to our good earth and America's well-being.

(*A long aside*: In 1971, DeMarco and I were writing our first book. Titled *Hard Tomatoes, Hard Times*, it was an exposé of how tax-paid agriculture research schools were using public funds for projects that benefited corporations at the expense of farmers, workers, consumers . . . and food itself. The title referred to those hard, pale tomatoes wrapped in plastic that supermarkets used to sell. Remember those tasteless nuggets? They were thrust upon us because California's agribusiness powers wanted to harvest their crop mechanically, rather than hiring farmworkers. Thus, in the late 1960s, the agriculture school at the University of California, Davis, dutifully produced a tomato harvester.

There was only one small problem: the machine crushed the tomatoes. So, the plant breeders at Davis, ever dutiful to corporate interests, returned to the lab, and—voilà!—they designed a hybrid tomato that was hard enough to withstand the machine's grasp. Even then, it had to be harvested green. But, hey, no problem. Just gas those babies with a ripening chemical and they'll turn pink enough to fool consumers into thinking the packages contain real tomatoes.

What a deal! Agribusiness got its machine and a machine-ready hard tomato at taxpayer expense—but within a couple of years after this technological "achievement" was introduced, five thousand small tomato farmers in California were put out of business by the mass-produced machine tomatoes, and some fifteen thousand farmworkers lost their harvesting jobs. Your tax dollars at work.

And what about consumers? Well, in the process of interviewing policy makers at the U.S. Department of Agriculture [USDA] for our book, DeMarco discovered that the agriculture research establishment relegated consumer concerns to the "little ladies" [remember: it's 1971] who taught home economics. Rarely were these women consulted when the plant breeders, engineers, and mechanics got together to "design" a food product.

The official line was that while the new machine-harvested tomato was not cheaper than nature's own, at least consumers could buy it year-round. In an interview with a USDA official, DeMarco commented that the off-season supermarket "tomatoes" she'd tried had no taste and—other than shape—bore no relationship to the luscious tomatoes she'd grown up with in New Jersey. The official—in a sincere, life-moves-on tone—dismissed this concern as a minor drawback: "Your children will never know the difference." *End of long aside.*)

Wrong. Even as he spoke, people were paying more attention, getting more concerned, and asking more questions than the aloof agribusiness power brokers could possibly imagine. A *food awakening* was already beginning to take hold. It's understandable that the establishment would have been clueless about this, since it was driven by ordinary people, not by "leaders" (nearly all of whom were in harness and pulling mightily for the industrial agriculture model) and not by the likes of today's Whole Foods empire (the company didn't exist when people began to move; it only came along later to ride the commercial wave of the awakening).

DeMarco and I were in touch with this emerging movement through our work in the 1970s as codirectors of a public interest group with the unwieldy name of Agribusiness Accountability Project. In addition to research and writing, we did a lot of speaking in cities around the country. Some of our friends were baffled that we were going into urban areas to raise what they assumed were farm issues: "Why are you talking about agriculture?"

We weren't. We were talking about *power*. We asked consumer-minded audiences, "If you can't even control what's in your dinner, what can you control? Who decided to take the flavor out of tomatoes? Why are breakfast cereal prices so high? Who says it's 'necessary' to dump eight billion pounds of pesticides every year on America's croplands, with the poisons contaminating the strawberries you give your kids as a treat?"

We were also talking about the emergence of a fledgling populist political alliance that had enormous potential to upset the best-laid plans of the food giants. Discussion of economic structure is usually a boring snore producer, but we found that people quickly and easily "got it" when we merely held up a box of Wheaties or a can of Campbell's soup, products that most people in the seventies had in their kitchens. We then described what these packages held for the following:

> *Farmers*: On average, only 18¢ of the consumer's food dollar goes to the farmer (there's less than a nickel's worth of wheat in Wheaties. The box costs more).
>
> *Farmworkers*: You could double the miserly wages they are paid and not raise the price of a can of soup even a penny.
>
> *Environment*: Saturating fields with pesticides every year is literally killing the soil and has contaminated nearly half of America's groundwater.
>
> *Energy*: With centralized agribusiness, the typical food product travels fifteen hundred miles to get to your supermarket, wasting massive amounts of fuel.
>
> *Consumers*: A handful of conglomerates monopolizes every aspect of the food economy, leaving consumers overcharged at the cash register and shortchanged on quality.

Let's see—farmers, labor, environmentalists, and consumers. Gosh . . . that's most of us! The Powers That Be work diligently to keep us divided, but if we could come together in a movement that involved us all, something big could happen.

And it is happening. Accelerating from the seventies, all parts of the movement have had their individual upchuck moments over the way the corporatized, industrialized, globalized food system is working, and they have been rebelling against it. Movements, however, don't spring forth full-grown.

> "If you find that you've dug yourself into a hole, the very first thing to do is stop digging."
>
> – Old Texas saying

Each part has to develop in its own way. In this case, the various parties had practically no connection, no awareness that all were seeking a better system. Although they had no central leaders, no road map or plan, they've gradually found their way by finding one another.

UP FROM THE GRASSROOTS

The result is an alternative food economy that has begun to flourish and a proud movement that is surging in popularity.

There are some eight thousand organic farmers today, producing everything from wheat to meat (and thousands more farmers are making the transition to organic).

Some facts about the organic food market include the following:

- Sales of organic food topped $17 billion in 2006 and are increasing at about 20 percent a year—ten times the rate of other foods.

- About 40 percent of American shoppers regularly buy some organic foods.

- Sales of organic beer (O, progress!) rose 40 percent in 2005. Such entrepreneurial leaders as Morgan Wolaver, the maker of a terrific line of organic brews sold under the Wolaver label, have established an expanding niche for beers made with organic ingredients. (*Disclosure*: I have done extensive consumer research into the quality of his suds, although I am not under the influence as I write this.)

- Direct sales from local farmers to consumers are booming through some four thousand vibrant farmers' markets in practically every city.

- Food co-ops (once the rather funky domain of hippies) are thriving, with about three hundred of them across the country, totaling $750 million a year in business and providing another way around the corporate system for local farmers, food artisans, and consumers.

- All levels of eateries—from white-tablecloth restaurants to Dot's Diner—not only feature organic foods on their menus, but also pride themselves on having locally produced, seasonal ingredients.

- Such major wholesalers as Sysco, practically all supermarket chains, and giants such as Costco and even Wal-Mart now realize that the demand is so strong that they have to carry some organic foods.

Oh, and those kids who "will never know the difference"? They've been in the lead of this movement from the start. In the seventies, it was college kids who became the founders of food co-ops, organic farms, and other enterprising efforts to get around that hard tomato. In the eighties and the nineties, it was young moms who asked, "What's in this stuff I'm feeding my kids?" and searched out better alternatives.

And today it's the kids and the grandkids of all of the previously mentioned kids who are helping to push good food into that last refuge of awful "mystery meats" and prepackaged fat bombs: the school cafeteria. The farm-to-cafeteria movement has received little coverage by the national media establishment, but it is spreading across the country. More than four hundred school districts and two hundred university cafeterias now build their daily menus around fresh, mostly organic ingredients bought from local farmers and food makers.

Also, prodded by the example of Alice Waters—the pioneering visionary and a tireless promoter of America's "good food" movement—many of the youngsters in these schools now grow some of their own food, as well as help to prepare and serve it, as part of a spreading "edible schoolyard" program. Some are even adopting a concept called "edible classroom," where food is used as an integral

ORGANIC LABOR

Even the weakest area of the movement's evolution—farm labor—is at last making gains. Jim Cochran, an organic strawberry grower near Santa Cruz, California, is a leader in pushing the movement to get this part right. He is the first organic farmer to sign a United Farm Workers Union contract with those who labor on his farm. It provides wages of $8 to $12 an hour, medical and dental care, a pension plan, and paid vacations. "Farmers need to see that it can be done," he said. "We need to go from saying 'I'm doing the best I can' to realizing that we should do more."

Michael Sligh, a third-generation farmer and the founding chairman of the National Organic Standards board, heads a coalition of farmers, farmworker advocacy groups, and others that is developing a social justice label for organic production. The foods will carry a sticker certifying that the producer meets the standards of fair treatment for workers, which includes providing decent wages, health care, and the right to unionize.

Like fair trade labels and the organic label itself, the social justice sticker will educate consumers, literally bringing home the message that labor issues are central to the very concept of "organic." Not only can social justice labeling help workers, but it will also help to distinguish the participating farmers from the Wal-Marts that are trying to muscle in on the organic trade.

The giants want to claim that their products are organic, even if they're grown in China under abominable labor conditions. The justice stickers up the ante on the global conglomerates, setting a standard of wholesomeness that their business model won't let them even try to achieve. It puts more power in the hands of consumers to shape the economy. As Sligh said, "Every time we go to the grocery store, we're choosing what kind of food system we want."

part of the curriculum, providing a tangible (and tasty) way to teach history, science, math, geometry, and other topics.

Just as good food springs from well-tended ground, so has this grassroots movement. No one in a position of power—political or economic—made any of these improvements happen. In a remarkably short time, ordinary Americans informed themselves, organized, and acted to assert their own values over those of the corporate structure. Family by family, business by business, they have changed not only the market but the culture. By taking charge of what goes on their plates, people are beginning to take charge of their lives.

CHAPTER 16

How We Live

On February 8, 2006, the food section of the *New York Times* ran
a correction for a recipe it had printed the week before. The
recipe was for chipotle meatballs, a Mexican dish, and the *Times* said
that it had misstated the amount of chipotle chiles to be used:

> It is one or two canned chiles.

> Not one or two cans.

Yeeeow!

For nearly all things in life, it is important to get the balance right.
In personal relationships, foreign policy, your golf swing, raising children, drinking beer, religion, work, and police power, balance matters.

Nowhere is this more true (or more dicey) than in humankind's
relationship with nature. And nowhere is the clash between corporate
values and human values playing out more dramatically today than in
the crucial battle over how our society will live on the land.

Let's say it bluntly: America's industrial presence has been brutish.
Corporations have treated nature as something either to be extracted

for profit or to be destroyed in order to get at the profit. The attitude has been: "Hey, if you're going to make lard, first you've got to boil a hog, so those who are squeamish about it should just cover their eyes and get the hell out of our way."

But a broad, deep, and powerful rebellion is pushing back . . . and a big change is coming. This is because we have learned about sprawling dead zones the size of states in our oceans and have seen rivers so laden with toxic chemicals that they catch on fire. We've experienced deadly floods and mudslides as a result of clear-cutting and the mindless destruction of marshes. We've found cancer clusters downwind from chemical plants and downstream from waste dumps. We have seen forests and crops destroyed by acid rain caused by smokestacks hundreds of miles away and have become asthmatic from the fumes of our own tailpipes. We receive frequent urgent warnings not to eat certain types of fish because they've been made toxic by industrial pollutants. And now we've discovered that we have a toxic stew of man-made chemicals and heavy metals coursing through our bodies. Every one of us! Witnessing all of this (and so awfully much more), a rising majority is deciding that the corporate ethic is suicidal.

The harsh lesson is that there are natural limits to what humans can do, and our society has arrogantly and blindly pushed right up against them. We don't need to learn to live with nature; we must recognize something far more basic: We *are* nature. We are finding out (often the hard way) that we cannot long abuse the natural environment without abusing ourselves.

In the case of global warming, our man-made environment has become catastrophically out of balance with the natural, causing Earth's thermostat to go on the fritz. Since the 1950s, gas emissions (primarily carbon dioxide) from our autos, utility plants, and other heavy industries have been building up in the atmosphere, trapping heat and leading to our steadily warming globe.

There's now a scientific consensus that the results—already well under way—will be near apocalyptic for the web of life on our planet: perverse weather patterns, more (and more intense) hurricanes, deadlier heat waves, prolonged and spreading droughts, melting glaciers, rising seas, falling water tables, disappearing species, and an increase in diseases.

If you whack yourself over the head with a ball-peen hammer, that's stupid. But to keep doing it—that's insane. And, of course, if you whack others with a ball-peen hammer, that's criminal.

As a society, America has been criminally insane. Our scientists have known for years what the greenhouse gas emissions are doing . . . and they've tried to tell us to stop it. But our political, industrial, media, and other leaders have been abject failures, even deliberately misleading the people on this growing crisis.

- *The coal operators, the utility executives, the auto barons, and the oil giants*—hooked on the status quo—literally have conspired to deny that global warming even exists.

- *The politicians* (with the exception of such occasional breakaways as Al Gore) have willfully worn blinders made of industry's campaign cash, so they see no evil and do exactly nothing.

- *The media powers*, bowing to advertiser dollars, stayed silent for years or actually ran stories pooh-poohing the emerging crisis, while also running endless ads for the biggest, baddest, most gas-guzzling, emission-spewing Hummer that industry could design.

In 2000, the political wet dream of the greenhouse gas emitters came true when Bush and Cheney were slipped into the White House. Even as the impact of global warming worsened, as the scientific warnings grew more insistent, and as the general public began to awaken, the Bushites kept their heads stuck in the tailpipes and the smokestacks of their industrial funders, working furtively to monkey wrench the

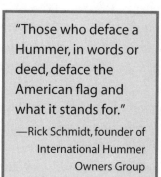

"Those who deface a Hummer, in words or deed, deface the American flag and what it stands for."

—Rick Schmidt, founder of International Hummer Owners Group

regulatory machinery to allow *more emissions*. George and Dick, two oil guys, are so tethered to the industry that they wouldn't admit that there's a crisis if their undershorts caught fire.

Luckily, contrary to Bush's assertion that he's "the decider," he's not. We are. And We the People not only have awakened to the looming threats of global warming, but are on the move to do something about it.

Some steps are being taking at the personal level. Many families are buying small, fuel-efficient cars, forcing even Detroit's dim-witted auto executives to notice. Children, moved to tears by the plight of polar bears drowning because their habitat is melting, are pushing for conservation and renewable energy in their schools and homes. Willie Nelson and others are tanking up their diesel vehicles with used vegetable oil from fast-food joints and are getting better mileage, smoother-running engines, and an exhaust that emits no toxins and smells like doughnuts. There's a boom in green culture: eco art, film fests, songwriting, weddings, and even a twenty-four-hour Planet Green cable-TV channel planned by Discovery.

This grassroots energy campaign is prompting city and state governments to respond with real actions. Cities (including our own Austin) are leading the way with serious commitments to wind power, solar installations, and plug-in hybrid cars. While Washington piddles with legislation to control auto emissions, twenty states have already passed their own emissions controls (overall, at least three hundred bills have been filed in forty states to address greenhouse gases and climate change). Prodded by environmental groups, Massachusetts and eleven other states sued George W.'s Environmental Protection Agency, leading to last year's landmark Supreme Court decision requiring the agency to start regulating greenhouse gas emissions. After a yearlong campaign by students in 2007, the ten-campus University of California system adopted a far-reaching "Environmental Sustainability Policy," which includes provisions to help reduce global warming.

Still, the industry and its political henchmen stall and squawk, dodge and dissemble, litigate and lobby, posture and prevaricate—anything and everything to maintain business as usual. In their long whine, they make two central claims:

1. *The Me-No-Pogo claim.* We have met the enemy, say the corporate chieftains . . . and it's not us. Or at least, you can't prove with 100 percent certainty that our pollution is causing this, so

no one should take any action until more research can be completed sometime in the misty, distant future. Meanwhile, if you get hot at Christmastime, just crank up your AC.

2. *The Chicken Little claim.* Good Lord almighty, don't you know what'll happen if you clamp down on CO_2 emissions? You'll turn Detroit into a ghost town, create a tsunami of job losses everywhere, bankrupt every utility, spark a national Depression, destroy the American lifestyle, unleash a plague of locusts, allow the terrorists to win, and cause the sky to fall.

First, the only thing that's 100 percent certain in science is that nothing is 100 percent certain. How about 90 percent? That's pretty conclusive. In the most authoritative scientific analysis yet done on global warming (marshalling the best research of 2,500 top scientists from 120 nations), the UN Intergovernmental Panel on Climate Change concluded last year, *with 90 percent certainty*, that the warming is caused by our cars and industrial activity.

Even if part of the warming is due to one of nature's eons-long cycles, we human types are pumping thirty-two billion tons of the gas that causes warming into the atmosphere each year. Earth has never before had to contend with this extra blast from us, and it can't be good for the balance of things.

Besides, what does it matter whether all the fault is our own? We can't fix nature's mysterious ways, but we can fix what we're doing. And we must. This really does happen to be a life-and-death matter, on a biblical level of devastation. It will affect all of our children and their children (not to mention every other species) if we don't respond PDQ. Scientists give us about ten years before the CO_2 buildup reaches an irreversible level. Knowing what we know, why wouldn't we act?

Oh, yeah, I forgot: the economic sky will fall if we do. Excuse me, but what a load of self-serving rat shit that is! No one's talking about doing anything that'll shut down the economy. We're just proposing to do energy differently and, in the process, make our economy more prosperous, democratic, secure, and healthy.

The utilities, the oil corporations, and the auto chieftains could have moved America in this direction years ago, averting the global warming crisis and creating a world of opportunities. But there are slugs with more adaptability, creativity, and get-up-and-go than these intractable behemoths. They can't save themselves, much less us.

Luckily, we need not stay shackled to them, for there are so many entrepreneurs, shade-tree mechanics, Web wonks, inventors, groups, mayors, and other innovators who are out here in America producing the alternatives for our CO_2-free, green future. Global warming, ironically, can be our ticket to real energy independence, based on retrofitting every building and home in our country for conservation, finding efficiency breakthroughs for solar energy and all other renewables, converting to clean auto technologies, connecting our population centers with high-speed trains, building passenger-friendly mass transit systems within our urban complexes, making it possible for more people to walk and bike, and . . . add your own idea!

Far from leading to job loss, such a proud national undertaking would be a job-creating wonder. Millions of machinists, construction

---

BLUE-GREEN

One way that corporate elites maintain their grasp on power is to pit us against each other. The classic example, which was very successful in the past, has been to cast environmentalists and workers as irreconcilable enemies. A development last year, however, puts the lie to the establishment's claim that any environmental advance is a loss for labor. United Steelworkers of America, our nation's largest manufacturing union (with 850,000 members), formed the Blue-Green Alliance with the Sierra Club, the nation's largest grassroots environmental group (750,000 members). The alliance has developed a joint public policy agenda, with the number one priority being the pursuit of clean energy. As the Steelworkers' feisty president, Leo Gerard, said, "Secure twenty-first-century jobs are those that will help solve the problem of global warming with energy efficiency and renewable energy."

workers, autoworkers, service employees, engineers, architects, computer programmers, and others who are being discarded by today's corporate system would be needed to build, maintain, and operate this new green infrastructure. These would be good jobs with good wages—middle-class opportunities restored.

I know that the rest of the world is fed up with America being so full of itself, but this really is an area where the United States has the responsibility to lead. On the one hand, our country is the top spewer of greenhouse gases and the world's biggest energy hog. But on the positive side, our nation has the wealth to lead this conversion, and our people have the can-do ethic for grabbing hold of what would be the biggest peacetime initiative since the New Deal and the Marshall Plan.

What we need is the political leadership to act. Alas . . . what we have is George W. He said last year that there's no use for America to step forward because "China will produce greenhouse gases that will offset anything we do in a brief period of time." (Thank God, he's not in charge of the fire department: "Well, we're not going to put out this fire, because another one will just pop up across town, so what's the use?")

Once again, the people have to be the leaders.

CHAPTER 17

A Mass Movement Arises

During his thirteen years as the CEO of ExxonMobil, Lee Raymond was paid $144,000. Not per year, of course . . . not per month . . . not per week. That's what he drew per day. A total of $686 million. Plus a car.

Then, when he retired in December 2005, instead of a gold watch, Exxon gave him a gold mine: a retirement package worth $400 million. Factor in this wad, and Raymond's total take as CEO adds up to *$28,000 an hour.* Maybe this is why the executive suite at Exxon headquarters in Houston is referred to internally as the "God Pod."

But this pay is ungodly. All the more so because Raymond's rich reward is for running a corporation that profits from polluting our air, water, bodies, and future. In addition to being responsible for such massive messes as oil spills (remember the *Valdez*), ExxonMobil is one of the world's top producers of the greenhouse gases that are contaminating Earth's atmosphere and warming our planet. To add insult to such catastrophic injury, this oil giant—on Raymond's watch—funneled millions of dollars into right-wing groups in a self-serving political effort to attack the scientific consensus that gas pollutants are a major cause of climate change. He also presided over the distribution of millions of dollars to assorted politicians who were willing to keep government from restraining the polluters.

Some CEOs like Raymond are getting so rich, they could afford to air-condition hell. And I'll tell you what: they'd better be setting some money aside for that project.

We can wait for heavenly intervention to cope with the corporate forces of environmental desecration, or we can step forward ourselves as a society to say, "¡Ya basta! Enough is enough!"

That's why a press conference held in Washington, D.C., on January 17, 2007, was so important, and even historic, for the unprecedented alliance that its participants represented. Maybe you didn't hear about it. That's because the media covered it as a mere curiosity, not comprehending the Big Story standing right in front of them. As is their fashion, the media whizzes gave the alliance a one-day run as a midlevel story before flitting off for yet another breathless report on Paris Hilton.

What they missed is the coming together of two of the most potent, most persuasive, and, one would assume, least compatible communities in America: scientists and evangelical Christians. Just as surprising (and exciting) is that this coalition was uniting around the issue of climate change. The press conference was convened to release a document—an "Urgent Call to Action"—signed by twenty-eight evangelical and scientific leaders.

The participants are not a ragtag bunch of fringe scientists and naïve seminarians. They are some of America's top scientists on climate issues, including Nobel laureates. And they are mainstream conservative leaders from the thirty-million-member evangelical churches of our country.

In the past, evangelicals have been taught that elite environmental scientists are, as one participant put it, "latte-sipping, Prius-driving, endive-munching, *New York Times*–reading, you know, snobs." On the other hand, intellectuals have a stereotype of evangelicals as "Hummer-driving, Bible-thumping, you know, fire-breathing, snake-handling fundamentalists."

What changed is that the two groups actually met face-to-face.

Spearheaded by Dr. Eric Chivian, a Nobel laureate biochemist at Harvard Medical School, and by the Reverend Richard Cizik, the director of governmental affairs for the National Association of Evangelicals, twenty-eight leaders from both communities held a retreat late in 2006 at a conference center in Thomasville, Georgia. Although Cizik believes that God created the Earth and all living creatures in six days, and while Chivian believes that the Earth and all living things have evolved over billions of years, they agreed not to focus on "the how" of creation, but on the "what now?"

They happily discovered far more concordance than any of them had expected, quickly moving beyond dialogue to what they call "a shared sense of moral purpose." Their call to action is not flinching in its assessment of the problems and not timid about confronting the status quo, as these excerpts show:

> "We agree not only that reckless human activity has imperiled Earth—especially the unsustainable and shortsighted lifestyles and public policies of our own nation—but also that *we share a profound moral obligation to work together* to call our nation, and other nations, to the kind of dramatic change urgently required in our day. . . .

> Each particular problem could be enumerated, but here it is enough to say that *we are gradually destroying the sustaining community of life on which all living things on Earth depend.* . . .

> We believe that the protection of life on Earth is a profound moral imperative. It addresses without discrimination the interests of all humanity as well as the value of the nonhuman world. It requires a new moral awakening to a compelling demand, clearly articulated in Scripture and supported by science, that *we must steward the natural world* in order to preserve for ourselves and future generations a beautiful, rich, and healthful environment. . . .

> We declare that every sector of our nation's leadership—religious, scientific, business, political, and educational—must

act now to work toward the fundamental change in values, lifestyle, and public policies required to address those worsening problems before it is too late. *There is no excuse for further delays.*

The fact that this coalition of religious and scientific leaders exists at all is remarkable, but its political significance is all the more exceptional because of the clarity, passion, and determination that unite them. All are people of prestige within their worlds, and all are breaking with convention to forge this odd-bedfellow alliance, as they risk derision and rebuke from their peers. Yet each one of them has stepped forward because of the urgency of this crucial issue and because they believe that their unique alliance will let them make the kind of difference that they can't make separately.

Dr. Joel Hunter is the senior pastor of the twelve-thousand-member Northland Church, which has five locations around Orlando, Florida. "I'm one of a growing number of local pastors who intends to do what is right in caring for God's creation," he said. "We are glad to be working with our friends in the scientific community. They have the facts we need to present to our congregations. We have the numbers of activists who will work through the church and the government and the businesses to make a significant impact."

Dr. Edward O. Wilson is America's most renowned scientist and an avowed secular humanist. Raised in Alabama, this two-time Pulitzer prize–winning author heads the Department of Evolutionary Biology at Harvard. "Science and religion," he said, "are the two most powerful social forces in the world. The so-called cultural wars between them needlessly blocked full cooperation between secular scientists and religious believers." Wilson said that the crisis of climate change can be dealt with and that the benefits "are beyond calculation," but that the forces profiting from the climate's destruction are enormously powerful. Thus, the need for uniting science with the churches: "At the end of the day, the direction we take will be an ethical decision. It will have to have a religious intensity."

One strong point of convergence between the empirical and the biblical that helped the two groups bond is that global warming is so rapidly destroying entire species. Scientists express it in terms of the destruction of essential biodiversity, while evangelicals see it as the destruction of the Creation. Either way, it is disastrous for life on Earth.

Both Dr. Wilson and Dr. Peter Raven, one of the world's leading botanists and the longtime director of the Missouri Botanical Garden, noted that if the human causes of global climate change continue unabated, *half* of Earth's current plant and animal species will be extinguished by the end of the century. "Species, of course, have become extinct regularly over the course of time," Raven said. "Today, however, the rate of extinction, for which we are responsible, is thousands of times faster than the rate at which new species originate, and that [extinction] rate is growing rapidly."

Dr. James Hansen, the head of the NASA Institute for Space Studies and an expert on Earth's changing climate, put it bluntly: "Climate change is happening. Animals know it. Many are trying to migrate to stay within their climate zone, but some are running out of real estate. They're in trouble." He added that by doing nothing about the CO_2 we're spewing into the atmosphere (a fourth of which stays there "forever," meaning the cumulative impact becomes irreversible), "we will create a different planet. We will destroy Creation."

> "The Lord God took the man and put him in the Garden of Eden to work it and take care of it."
>
> —Genesis 2:15

On the religious side, the Scriptures abound with clear mandates for humans to be not just takers of God's bounty but to be its *caretakers* as well. As Reverend Cizik said, "Obviously, as evangelicals, we believe that God will judge us if we destroy—through the loss of biodiversity, human-induced climate change, and the like—the Creation. And therefore, we as evangelicals have a special obligation, a duty of stewardship, to be more vigilant in fact than others."

Yes, but the right-wing Christian political establishment has turned environmentalism into a bogeyman in so many of the forty-five thousand evangelical churches across the country, demonizing environmentalists as tree-hugging pagans who worship the Creation rather than the Creator. How can this new alliance hope to break through such a barrier?

By staying within the culture, within the Bible itself (which one of the scientists in the coalition referred to as "this very green book"). Dr. Cheryl Johns, a Pentecostal preacher and a professor of discipleship at the Church of God Theological Seminary in Cleveland, Tennessee, answered in some detail: "First it is a matter of transforming the affections, of teaching our people that love of Creation is an extension of the love of God. Second, it is a matter of transforming lifestyles and values, creating awareness that conservation and stewardship is part of the Christian life and witness. And third, it is a matter of transforming Christian theology, raising awareness that God's mission to save people is part of God's intention to restore all of Creation. Finally, it is a matter of educating for justice and compassion, realizing that it is the poor of the world that are most acutely affected by global climate change." The educational task is a prophetic one, she said, compelling Christians "to speak with urgency and passion regarding our vocation as caretakers of God's beautiful and glorious world."

Reverend Hunter added a pragmatic note, saying that he and others are putting together a "pastor's tool kit" on global warming. It will have biblical references, resources, action steps for individuals, ten things to do as a church, and so forth. The reverend said, "We are posturing this packet for skeptics, and we expect that. But even as we say that, we're not facing an ignorant people here. We're facing people who are open, who will be willing to learn. There are very, very few Christians who are not at least open to the facts, and when they understand the facts, then they're on board.

"And that's why we need the partnership with the scientific community, because it makes that pastoral leadership credible. With that broad leadership there will be a very, I think, quick turnaround on this issue. This is one of those issues that's not going to take a long learning curve. If people are given what they can do, and it's from a personal and a church and a community and a national constructive manner, then they're going to respond."

CHAPTER 18

Flowers in the Field

I f you stroll down West Mary Street in South Austin, you might
come across a surprising sight on the front porch of a small house.
A mountain goat. He's Nik, the beloved pet of Joel Muñoz, a semi-
retired appliance repairman. Nik has lived at this address on West
Mary for years, bothering no one and amusing many. But in 2005, a
couple of newcomers to the neighborhood complained to the city
about an "unauthorized" animal.

Sure enough, Nik was in violation of an ordinance prohibiting
livestock from living within a hundred feet of any neighbor's house.
Muñoz was ticketed and given ten days to get rid of the offending
goat.

South Austinites, however, have a pretty spunky attitude (the
area's unofficial slogan is, "We're all here because we're not all
there"), and when word spread that Nik had been nipped by the law,
a citizens' rebellion erupted. E-mails flew, city council members
were confronted, and petitions were circulated to spare the goat.

Taken aback by the outcry, city officials scrambled to find a way
out. Finally, bowing to public pressure, the mayor himself had to step

in and take extraordinary action. He issued an official pardon to Nik and publicly declared him "a good goat." So, if you're ever on West Mary Street, stop by and give Nik a thumbs-up.

When you see how people respond to small injustices, it should come as no surprise that when folks finally absorb the truth about huge outrages, they are transformed. Beyond the hard work of such big enviro organizations as the Sierra Club and Friends of the Earth, the history of America's emerging environmental majority is replete with people experiencing their own personal awakenings and responding with spontaneous outbursts of outreach and activism. This flowering in the field mostly happens beneath the radar of the national media establishment, but it is the true hope for a green Earth.

The blossoming of an evangelical environmentalism—Creation Care, as they choose to call it—promises to add a constituent strength and a moral suasion to the environmental movement that could not have been imagined a decade ago, and it is changing the political landscape. The Thomasville gathering is but one part of this arising. Stories abound from all across the country, as Christians have come to realize through various epiphanies that to live their values, they are going to have to buck the corporate order and be a force for change. A couple of examples:

CHRISTIANS FOR THE MOUNTAINS

Some people have environmentalism thrust upon them by discovering that their children are being sickened by a nearby toxic facility, for example, or learning that a chemical plant is going to be built in their neighborhood, or waking up to hear bulldozers as developers take out the community's woods. But few have had a more god-awful awakening than the people of our Southern Appalachian Mountains.

There is environmental degradation—and then there is *environmental degradation*. The latter punches you in the stomach, knocks you to your knees, and leaves you gasping in disbelief. A coal company practice called "mountaintop removal" (MTR) falls in this category.

Let's start with what they are degrading. The Appalachians of West Virginia and Eastern Kentucky are the oldest mountain range in

America. No adjectives are adequate to describe the serene, ancient beauty you see, hear, smell, taste, and feel in these mountains. This is a remote and rugged expanse of high razorback ridges, plunging down into deep and dark valleys (called "hollers") and forested by an unparalleled diversity of mature broadleaf trees that have an Appalachian ancestry going back nearly three hundred million years. Pristine creeks, streams, and waterfalls run through this region, and uncountable species of flowers, fish, woodland animals, birds, and other living creatures call it home.

Mountain people call it home, too. And they have a deep tie to this place that is the stuff of songs, legends, and history. Their culture is a rich mix that derives from the Shawnees, the Creeks, the Choctaws, and the Cherokees who populated these mysterious mountains for centuries; the Scotch-Irish, who came in the 1730s; and later arrivals, including Germans and escaped slaves. Because of the enveloping, insular nature of the Appalachians, people here have retained their ethnic traditions and blended them to produce a music, a religion, a spirit, and an attitude that are unique.

If you're the honcho of a coal corporation, however, you look at this special place and see: Black gold! Money! Riches to grab! For generations, this impoverished region has been mined, with billions of dollars' worth of coal taken out by tunneling down into the mountains or boring in from the sides. Coal has built fortunes for faraway investors, while the miners have barely gotten paid enough to eke out a hard living. But people stay in this special place, grateful that at least they have their mountains.

Until now. Until mountaintop removal. This nifty process—first developed about thirty-five years ago, but only used extensively since the 1990s—allows corporations to extract the coal much more cheaply, employing far fewer workers. Actually, "removal" is much too delicate a term for this abhorrent, totally destructive assault on Mother Nature. Behold:

> First, the corporations scalp the mountains, clear-cutting the old oaks and other hardwood trees, then bulldozing them into huge piles and burning them as trash.

Second, they scrape off the ancient forest floor down to the bedrock, removing all topsoil, plant life, and organisms and shoving this mass over to the side of the mountain.

Third, the big booms come. Holes are drilled down into the bedrock, then filled with the same volatile mixture that Timothy McVeigh detonated in Oklahoma City—only the typical MTR blast is ten times the force of that one (three million pounds of explosives are used every day for MTR in West Virginia's mountains alone). The blasts literally decapitate a mountain, reducing its top third to rubble.

Fourth, the rubble, topsoil, and all else that had been the mountain's top is now labeled "spoil." Do the companies haul it away? Heavens, no! That would cost money. Instead, they "remove" it by crudely, carelessly, shockingly, disgustingly shoving the waste down the side of the mountain into the valley below. Like a massive man-made landslide, the shoved spoil buries streams, fish, other animals, trees, habitat, and anything else in its path. The dumped residue rises hundreds of feet from the valley floor, and, at this point, instead of being called spoil, it acquires a new, almost bucolic name: "valley fill."

Fifth, with the mountain now suitably reconfigured to expose the seams of coal, the corporations bring in machines to scoop out the only part of the mountain that they value.

What we have here is *ecocide*: the total annihilation of a priceless ecosystem that is older than the Himalayas. The industry has a glib phrase that sums up its destructive process: "shoot and shove." More than twelve hundred square miles of mountains have already been shot and shoved—an area equal to a quarter-mile-wide strip running from New York City to San Francisco. More than a thousand miles of streams have been buried, a stretch of waterways longer than the Ohio River.

All of this is done so that the corporations can sell coal for $1-a-ton cheaper than if they mined it responsibly.

Aw, say the coal corporations, no harm done, since we do a reclamation job on the mountains after the coal is extracted. "Some of the sites are so beautifully reclaimed, many people can't tell the difference," gushed the president of the National Mining Association in 2004. Well . . . uh . . . actually, sir, one little difference people might notice is that the top third of the mountain is gone. Then there's all that spoil down in the creeks and valleys.

> When MTR was first being pushed into federal law back in 1973, Jennings Randolph, then a U.S. Senator from the Mountain State, explained to his colleagues why it was a good thing: "In the state of West Virginia, we have a need for level land."

As for reclamation, what was a tree-covered mountain peak now is a treeless mesa planted in patches of nonnative grass that struggles to survive in the lifeless shale that remains. Sometimes, the companies stock the flattened top with deer, which, under the law, lets them call their devastation a "wildlife habitat." One enthusiastic industry spokesman even tried to claim that an MTR mine planned in Mount Alpha, West Virginia, would improve people's view: "Right now, all they're looking at is trees. When we're done, they can look over and see grass and animals running. That's a whole lot prettier than trees."

From out of the dark depths of this dismal destruction, however, some bright lights are shining. Just as this region's poor mine workers once rose up to battle greedy coal barons and corrupt politicians to establish unions and gain a modicum of economic fairness, so are today's Appalachian people daring to stand up to those same corporate and political powers, which are now busy destroying these hallowed mountains. Tenacious groups like Kentuckians for the Commonwealth, Ohio Valley Environmental Coalition, and the West Virginia Highlands Conservancy have been battling the bastards in court, in public forums, in political campaigns, in the statehouses, in street demonstrations . . . and, now, *in church.*

Judy Bonds, whose family has been in these mountains for ten generations, is one of the longtime environmental leaders against MTR who has brought her faith to the cause. "I wonder," she asked, "which one of these mountains do you think God would come down here and blow up? Which one of these hollers do you think Jesus would store waste in?"

Bonds was raised a Christian, then strayed, but mountaintop removal brought her back. "It was the unjustness that I saw. And I began to pray for help. For guidance." She didn't merely pray and wait for deliverance, however; she's been a determined organizer and coalition builder through a group she heads, Coal River Mountain Watch. And a big part of her coalition-building against MTR these days is among the area's many church people.

Allen Johnson, a librarian in Dunmore, West Virginia, sings and plays in his church's band, but his most passionate singing is for biblical stewardship in Southern Appalachia. He cofounded and now directs a growing volunteer organization called Christians for the Mountains, reaching out to ministers and congregations to join the fight against MTR. In a recent Bill Moyers PBS documentary titled *Is God Green?* Johnson explained the moral rational for church engagement:

> Our theological thrust comes from Psalms 24:1. Basically, it says that the Earth and everything in it is God's property. We humans have the privilege to use it, but only with the corresponding responsibility to take good care of it and share it. Mountaintop removal mining and associated abuses ravage the land and impoverish the people for corporate greed.
>
> [They're] breaking a covenant with God . . . breaking a covenant with Creation and other people and future generations. It is a sin. Sin is not a word that is popular today, but that's what it is. S-I-N.

In Appalachia's small towns, Christian churches are at the center of community life. Enlisting them in activist opposition to MTR would build a formidable force—a majority force. In these churches and in the larger community, the majority already seems to be revolted by this corporate desecration. But it's not always easy or quick to translate personal revulsion into open revolt.

Not for nothing is the industry called "King Coal." Appalachia remains one of the most impoverished places in our country, and coal's executives have kept the people dependent on them for jobs and a tax base for public services. As Johnson said, "We are basically told, 'This is your economy. Take it or leave it. If you don't have coal, you'll have nothing. You'll be even more impoverished than you are now.' And, so, people are in a sense held hostage by the coal industry."

Many churches are captive, too. Preachers look to coal companies for donations to their building funds. Some of the churchgoers work for the company or their relatives do. The politicians who attend services count on getting campaign contributions from the company. In a company town, it's easy to become a company church.

Yet coal officials and their apologists can't directly assail the biblical and moral message that Christians for the Mountains is spreading, so instead they try to demonize Bonds, Johnson, and others as being in league with unholy nature worshippers. The corporate interests warn church leaders to avoid any activism that boosts nature's welfare by interfering with the area's wealth creator. After all, said a pious spokesman for the industry's lobbying group, "human welfare depends on the rational exploitation of nature." What's "rational," of course, is defined by the corporations, and their definition most certainly includes blowing up mountains.

The coal giants are even unabashed about citing God for their profiteering purposes. Moyers reported that when three hundred million gallons of toxic coal slurry from a mountaintop mine burst out of its dam in West Virginia to flood the valley and stream below (killing more than a million fish), a coal official shrugged it off as an "act of God."

But while Appalachian evangelicals might be financially beholden to the industry, they're not fools, and trying to indict the Creator for causing the "collateral damage" of mountaintop removal only backfires on King Coal. Carmelita Brown, who lives downhill from a mountaintop mine in Rawl, West Virginia, told Moyers in plain words, "God doesn't destroy the Earth. The coal companies is the ones that's destroying the Earth. So that's my opinion on that."

It's not her only opinion, either. Pointing up to a mountain peak where a powerful coal boss built a mansion for all the locals to see, Ms. Brown said, "To me, it's like he made a statement. You know? He's God. God on the mountain. But he's as close to God as he's going to get up on that mountain."

Luscious Thompson, a sixty-three-year-old former miner who lives in the Kentucky coal town of McRoberts, is also unimpressed with the corporate claim that coal's calamities come from the hand of God. He pointed to the horizon above his town that had been marked by a beautiful line of mountain peaks. They have since been "removed," along with the surrounding woods where he hunted. Now, when a good rain falls, runoff from the decapitated and stripped mountains floods into McRoberts. "I've been flooded three times since they started working on the mountaintop," Thompson said. "The coal company says it's God's will. Well, God ain't ever run no bulldozer."

TENDING THE GARDEN

Surprise, Karl! The very group that Bush politico Karl Rove counted on to provide the margin of victory for George W. in his presidential elections is now wandering off the fenced-in reservation he designed for them. Rove, along with such right-wing Christian political extremists as James Dobson and Pat Robertson, had rallied evangelical preachers from coast to coast around a couple of narrow, hot-button issues, particularly gay marriage and abortion.

But—oops!—now Karl and his right-wing Christian cronies are learning that evangelicals are not one-dimensional or as easily manipulated as Rove thought. Rove succeeded in politicizing these churches for 2004, but, to his dismay, they don't see themselves continuing as a punch-button GOP voting bloc. They're developing their own political agenda, which clashes mightily with the plutocratic ambitions of the Republicans' corporate base.

Instead of using a single-issue litmus test for deciding how evangelicals should vote, many leaders and individual pastors are searching their souls, re-searching their Bibles, and gradually stepping forth on such broad concerns as poverty, racial injustice, peace,

human rights, and environmentalism, all of it grounded in Scripture.
Barbara Williams-Skinner, who heads
a Christian training center in Tracy's
Landing, Maryland, was greeted
with a standing ovation at a March
2005 meeting of the National Association of Evangelicals when she pled
for churches to focus broadly on
issues of justice: "The litmus test is
the Gospel, the *whole* of it."

> When Reverend Peter Illyn, who heads an evangelical group in Washington State, took his family hiking in the Cascade Mountains, his eight-year-old son said to him, "Daddy, it's easy to believe in God when you're in the mountains."

For the White House and its corporate sponsors, the most stunning
shift has been the move by conservative churches to take on the polluters of our Earth. Out in Idaho, longtime environmental writer
Rocky Barker told Bill Moyers about a recent pastoral convert to Creation Care. Tri Robinson is the senior pastor of a Nazarene church
named Vineyard Boise, now with three thousand weekly attendees
congregating in a renovated supermarket building. Barker said that
Robinson would appear to be an almost stereotypical evangelical
preacher, having been a strong Bush supporter. "He's an avowed creationist. He's very pro-life. He's against gay marriage. He's a traditional Republican evangelical. Except now he's, uh—green."

In some fifteen years at Vineyard, Robinson never preached a
word on environmental responsibility—hardly a surprise in this
region of logging, mining, and ranching, where environmentalists
have been caricatured as the job-stealing spawn of Satan. But there's
another, awe-inspiring force at work in this part of the country:
nature. This is a wilderness state, where the jaw-dropping beauty of
mountains, snowy plateaus, high forests, white-water rivers, spectac-
ular sunsets, and starry nights form a natural cathedral. Just being in
places like Idaho can leave you feeling blessed to be even a small part
of the larger creation.

Robinson said that from his youth onward, he had valued his connection to nature, even living off the land for a while with his wife,
Nancy, on a Southern California ranch that had no electricity. "But

later in life," he said, "when I became a Christian and entered the ministry, somehow I disconnected from all of these values and affections. I never stopped loving nature, but it was somehow set aside because there was no real value for environmental stewardship in the church."

He added, "I was always afraid to use the word 'environment' because I didn't want to be labeled a 'liberal.'"

Yet Robinson kept seeing the beauty of creation all around him, kept reading almost daily about the desecration of that creation, and kept running across the biblical passages demanding that humans "tend the garden." Finally, he could no longer maintain the disconnect: "I realized I couldn't let political affiliation dissuade my higher allegiance to God's Kingdom. I said, 'I've got to do something about this.'"

He decided to preach. In the nonevangelical world, delivering an environmental message from the pulpit is commonplace, but doing it in a devoutly conservative place like Vineyard Boise Church wasn't only rare, it was unheard of. It literally required a leap of faith on Robinson's part.

"I prepared for about six months, meditating, praying, studying," he said. "I wanted to present this to [the congregation] straight from the Bible, because I knew if they could see it in the Bible, being primarily a solid evangelical church, that they would recognize the credibility at that point." In the spring of 2005, Pastor Robinson delivered his first environmental sermon and was stunned by the reaction of his congregation: a standing ovation. It seems that his church members had quietly been harboring many of the same thoughts about the natural world, and when Robinson dared to express them, they felt freed.

This was not to be a onetime sermon, for he has kept coming back to the message, and Vineyard's members have made a church-wide commitment to the mission of stewardship, putting it at the core of their spiritual and personal lives. "Our pastor really embraced the idea that Earth is a gift to all of us to use, enjoy, and protect," said one church member. "He presented the idea, the church embraced it, and we're doing it. This is something each person can do."

Some of their efforts are enviro baby steps (recycling, tree-plantings, energy conservation), but they represent a sea change in attitude, and when three thousand dedicated churchgoers in Boise are saying and doing something, it begins to ripple through the area. It makes a difference. What's happened in Robinson's church is a sincere awakening, giving rise to a scripturally based green morality that has already linked Vineyard members to Idaho's environmental movements, with personal connections that bring two sides onto the same side in an important cause.

Robinson himself has abandoned all reticence about speaking out, now saying bluntly, "We have wrongfully assumed that creation exists for our own consumption." He not only talks about local actions, but has also joined America's swelling evangelical chorus on the need for action against global warming. "For the Christian who cares about Earth and humanity, it is essential that we don't put our heads in the sand on this very crucial phenomenon. . . . For some reason, the environment has landed in the liberal camp and, because of it, many Christian leaders are afraid to embrace it. If we are to bring change, we must see this for what it is and take a stand for what is biblical and right."

In his 2007 book *Saving God's Green Earth*, Robinson makes clear that he's no longer in lockstep with Rove's Republicanism: "Many people perceive the church as conservative and therefore intimately allied with the Republican Party, which is more interested in capitalistic strength than environmental stewardship when it comes to managing our beautiful country. One environmentalist remarked in

Rick Johnson, the executive director of the Idaho Conservation League, told the *Boise Weekly* in 2005 that Vineyard's faith-based conservation initiative was a most welcome development: "The greatest threat to the environment is a lack of community, and faith groups promote community. When people are disconnected from each other, they can be disconnected from the physical world. But, together, communities take care of their gardens."

obvious irony: 'It's interesting that conservatives are the least likely to support conservation.' I believe it's time Christians begin to rediscover the values we have lost and be on the leading edge of promoting environmental stewardship."

One final thought from Robinson's book:

> The moment is right for the church to reverse its wrongs in the area of environmental stewardship. By abandoning our shortsighted thinking and returning long-term vision to the church, Christians have an opportunity to change things. It won't be easy. Many people from both liberal and conservative camps alike are likely to cast a suspicious eye on such a sudden reversal of position. But if the statistics are true and one-third of the world is comprised of Christians, what would happen if one-third of the world became serious about upholding the value of environmental stewardship?

CHAPTER 19

The Conscience of an Evangelical

On a flight in 2005, I was thumbing through the airline's onboard travel magazine and came across this letter to the editor:

> During a tour of the Grand Palace in Bangkok, I approached a monk, pointed to my camera, and asked if I could take his picture. He nodded . . . and posed standing very proud and upright. A young boy was selling bottled water nearby, so I bought two bottles and gave one to the monk. I paid the child and waited for my change. When it didn't come, I pointed to my palm, saying, "Don't I get change?" The child looked at the monk, then at me, and said in perfect English, "Change comes from within."

Reverend Rich Cizik is one who has looked within himself and found the strength to become a spirited exponent of a very big change within America's evangelical churches. He has been a key force in the churches' spreading awakening to both the reality of climate change and the biblical imperative to do something about it.

Cizik is well-placed to be an effective advocate, although his position would seem to be the last place you'd find a boat-rocker. For twenty-six years, he has run the Washington office of the National Association of Evangelicals (NAE). In essence, he's the chief legislative strategist and lobbyist for the association's fifty-nine denominations, forty-five thousand churches, and thirty million believers.

In a wide-ranging interview in his D.C. office near the Capitol Building, Cizik told me that global warming had not been any sort of priority for the NAE (pro or con), nor had he personally paid more than passing attention to it over the years. But, in 2002, he was almost literally dragged to a conference on climate change in Oxford, England.

The person doing the dragging was another evangelical, Reverend Jim Ball. This forty-six-year-old grew up as a Southern Baptist in suburban Dallas and attended a Baptist seminary in Kentucky. He had dismissed environmentalism as unimportant to his ministry, until a fellow theological student pointed him to the biblical message that Christian reconciliation is not merely about humans but *all* living things. By the mid-1990s, Ball had become one of the earliest evangelizers for Creation Care, with a special passion for awakening people to the catastrophic impacts of global warming. In 2000, he became the head of a pioneering group, the Evangelical Environmental Network, and he rose to national attention in 2003 when he and his wife, Kara, drove across the South in their blue hybrid Prius on an attention-getting preaching tour under the deliberately provocative banner of "What Would Jesus Drive?"

Cizik knew Ball, of course. He later said of him, "Jim is like one of the Old Testament prophets warning people. I'm sure he has wondered if he was ever going to see the day when the evangelical world was going to wake up." In 2002, when Ball asked him to go to the Oxford gathering of the Intergovernmental Panel on Climate Change (IPCC), Cizik was one of those asleep. "We have no dog in this fight," he told Ball. "Keep me out of this." Ball was persistent. "Come," he said, "at least listen."

Cizik went. He listened. He absorbed. He was moved. Then he took a walk in the gardens of Blenheim Palace at the invitation of the man who had chaired the IPCC meeting, Sir John Houghton. He's one of the world's leading climatologists, as well as a lifelong Christian who believes that the laws of science are the way God runs the universe. In other words, he speaks both science and Christian. "I'm telling you what is happening," the scientist told Cizik. "And I trust that God will speak to your heart. The fate of Earth may well depend on how Christians, especially evangelical Christians who take the Bible seriously, respond to the issues of climate change."

Referring to Genesis 2:15, the holy admonition to take care of the garden, Houghton said, "Richard, if you have decided that we are right about the facts, you cannot walk away from this conference and not do something." It was an altar call for Cizik: "I was hit right in the forehead with the facts. And I literally said to myself, God! How can anybody who believes the facts are thus not speak out?!"

FIRST STEPS

Reverend Cizik has not held his long-tenured position in the volatile worlds of church politics and Washington lobbying by being rash. As excited as he was by his epiphany in Oxford, he mulled it over and considered his path. He knew that many of his peers considered environmentalism to be the domain of godless liberals. "Don't go there," was the curt advice of the friends he consulted. But that wasn't a possibility once he'd seen the light. It was a matter of how to go there. He grounded himself in the issues of climate change and began a campaign of persuasion within the NAE, while also starting to speak about the issue publicly.

The first formal expression of the creation theology that he, Jim Ball, and others were developing came on October 7, 2004, when the NAE's board of directors unanimously adopted a twenty-six-page statement on public policy. Titled "For the Health of the Nation: An Evangelical Call to Civic Responsibility," it formally expanded the political focus of the association far beyond the strict agenda of marriage and abortion. "We seek justice and compassion for the poor and vulnerable," was one of the seven policy goals set forth, as were "We work to protect human rights" and "We seek peace and work to restrain violence." But the big breakthrough was the inclusion of a section titled "We labor to protect God's creation." It was the first-ever environmental declaration by the evangelical body, and it was surprisingly straightforward:

> We affirm that God-given dominion is a sacred responsibility to steward the Earth and not a license to abuse the creation of which we are a part. We are not the owners of creation, but its stewards, summoned by God to "watch over and care for it." This implies the principle of sustainability: our uses of the Earth must be designed to conserve and renew the Earth rather than to deplete or destroy it. . . . Because clean air, pure water, and adequate resources are crucial to public health and civic order, government has an obligation to protect its citizens from the effects of environmental degradation. . . . We urge government to encourage fuel efficiency, reduce pollution, encourage sustainable use of natural resources, and provide for the proper care of wildlife and their natural habitats.

It was the sure hand of Cizik that brought this to fruition. He was one of seven on the committee to draft it, but his most important contribution was being someone inside the NAE who really cared about the issue, who would shepherd the process, sell it within the whole movement, and get a hundred evangelical leaders to sign it.

The declaration, of course, was just the start. "Our strategy is leader to leader to leader," he said. "If you have fifty-nine denominations saying we endorse this, and they say to their pastors we endorse this, and the pastors endorse it to their Sunday school teachers—then that's how you start a movement."

Cizik also knew that while he was working downward through the system, another force of change was coming upward from the grassroots: young people. "It is becoming very apparent that the old guard, the religious right, is not going to meet the standards of the younger generation. That's everybody under fifty. Evangelicals under fifty are of the opinion that all of the principles matter. Not just some—not just the sanctity of human life or protecting traditional family—but all of them: human rights, justice for the poor and oppressed, peacemaking, and then this very controversial [Imagine that! Controversial!] Creation Care."

Then came the scientists. Or, actually, then came a cup of coffee. In 2005, a lady who doesn't want her name publicized (a story can't be good without a touch of mystery) telephoned Cizik and asked whether he'd join her for coffee. He would. He did. She'd heard some of the things he was saying about climate change and Creation Care and wanted him to meet her friends. One of her friends was Dr. Eric Chivian, the head of the Center for Health and the Global Environment at Harvard Medical School.

Cizik and Chivian hit it off, and in the course of their developing friendship, they realized that they represented a potentially potent political collaboration. "The scientists have the facts and we have the activists," Cizik said. "Now that's a one-two punch."

Thus was born the Thomasville meeting of those twenty-eight scientists and evangelicals, which Chivian sums up in one sentence: "We discovered that we were both speaking from our hearts and our minds, that we really liked each other, that we were there because we shared a very deep and profound concern for what was happening to the Creation, to the global environment, and that we had an enormous sense of urgency that the general public and our political leaders were not understanding, and that whatever differences we might have on some issues, we had to focus on the things we passionately agreed upon."

Okay, it's a *long* sentence, but the camaraderie, cohesiveness, and commitment it expresses promise to change the politics of global warming. Cizik put it this way: "I daresay that any Republican who has the audacity to stand up today, in light of all the facts that have come together, to say that climate change is a hoax—I daresay that politician will be in trouble with sizable numbers of evangelicals."

FORCES OF DARKNESS

Reverend Cizik is not the only one to realize that having evangelicals charged up about climate change creates a new political dynamic. Progressives, sadly, have not yet grasped the significance, but corporate polluters have, and their political apologists are on the attack, trying not only to discredit Cizik, but to force him out of the NAE.

Luckily, the attackers are morons. All right, all right. Maybe they're not morons, but they certainly do great impersonations of morons.

Back in the summer of 2006, James Dobson, the right-wing Republican political operative who heads Focus on the Family, wailed that Cizik is being divisive by pressing an agenda that is "anticapitalistic" and that reflects "an underlying hatred for America." Televangelist Pat Robertson weighed in with the accusation that Cizik is letting himself be "used by the radical left to further their agenda." In case you're unclear about what the left's global warming agenda is, Pat went on to explain it to his audience: "They want to shut America down. They just want to shut our industries down and put people out of work. And if need be, we'll have a long, cold winter where we'll all be freezing."

The lead attack dog, however, has been Senator Jim Inhofe, the oil-soaked Oklahoma Republican who chaired the U.S. Senate Committee on Environment and Public Works until the Republicans lost the Senate in 2006. He has made a career of carrying water for big greenhouse gas emitters, and they have stuffed his political pockets with nearly $1.5 million since he's been in Congress. Inhofe has returned the favor by being a ferocious denier that man-made global warming even exists, calling it "the greatest hoax ever perpetrated on the American people."

Hizzoner the Senator has assailed Cizik as being in a conspiracy with people who worship "the creeping things, the four-legged beasts, the birds and all that. That's their god."

On Miles O'Brien's CNN television show, Inhofe was asked about evangelicals becoming active on climate change issues. "Not at all. Not at all true," the senator blurted. "There's one individual. His name is Richard Cizik. He's the guy that's out there. And you talk about making money, there's a guy that's on the cutting edge, being sponsored by all these environmental groups to try to break into the National Association of Evangelicals. They [NAE officials] have rejected him and what he has said. He's speaking on his own, not for evangelicals."

Phew! Save some of that breath for breathing, Senator. First, Cizik has received neither money nor any other kind of sponsorship from enviro groups. Second, remember that NAE's board *unanimously* adopted the "Health of the Nation" document in 2004, including its powerful policy statement on Creation Care. Third, on this issue, Cizik seems to be speaking for nearly two-thirds of evangelicals: a March 2006 poll found that 63 percent of evangelicals say climate change is real and America must act now to deal with it.

Inhofe, however, is not one to let facts get in the way of a good attack. One of his efforts has been to go after Cizik in meetings with other lobbyists and evangelical

> How loopy is Inhofe? He told FOX News that the Weather Channel is behind the public's rising concern about climate change: "It's all about money. I mean, what would happen to the Weather Channel's ratings if all of the sudden people weren't scared anymore?"

leaders. "I just came from this incredible meeting," one of Rich's long-time lobbying colleagues told him in a phone call. "I've never seen anything like it. Inhofe went on about you for forty-five minutes."

The blatherings of the senator haven't really fazed Cizik, but he has been disappointed in some of his lobbying friends. "None of them in the room stood up to the U.S. senator and said, 'I know this person. He's been my friend for years and he's not who you say he is!' Nobody stood up! And I said to some of them, 'Why can't you?'

"And they said, 'Well, he's a senator.' What? Do you have no courage?"

After the January press conference with the scientists, the attack strategy went from trying to undermine Cizik to trying to take his job away from him. Just before the NAE's 2007 board meeting, a letter signed by such right-wing political figures as Dobson, Gary Bauer (the former GOP presidential candidate), Tony Perkins (not the actor in *Psycho* but the head of the Family Research Council), and Paul Weyrich (the longtime Republican strategist and leader of the far-right American Values group) was sent to the board and was released to the media.

"We have observed that Cizik and others are using the global warming controversy to shift the emphasis away from the great moral issues of our time," they wrote. And what would those issues be? Abortion and same-sex marriage, they explained—that is, the very issues used by Karl Rove to keep evangelicals on the GOP reservation. In an interview, Perkins added that Cizik is engaged in "a concerted effort to shift the focus of evangelical Christians to these issues that draw warm fuzzies from liberal crusaders."

He's diverting NAE's purpose and dividing its members, the signers complained, so "we respectfully suggest he be encouraged to resign."

NAE board members did no such thing. In fact, they gave Cizik the biggest show of support possible by simply making no response at all to the resignation demand, as though it had never existed. Instead, the board once again voted unanimously to affirm its 2004 vote for the "Health of the Nation" declaration and had Rich deliver the keynote address at the board's banquet, where he was warmly applauded.

PROBING CIZIK

Who is this guy, this born-again evangelical who is causing such consternation among big-time right-wing politicos? Who is this insider who has gone outside to forge an unprecedented alliance to advance the environmental cause? This comfortable church official is willing to take such personal and professional risks that some colleagues have lamented, "Rich, he's gone nuts!"

Cizik was raised on a farm in eastern Washington State. The family had a cherry orchard near Wenatchee and a dryland farm near Moses Lake. His mother, a schoolteacher, voted Democratic, while his farmer father voted Republican. "We always had battles at home," Rich said.

He went to Whitworth College in Spokane, got a Scottish Rite Fellowship for a master's degree in international affairs at George Washington University, and had a Rotary fellowship to study Mandarin in Taiwan. While at a Rotary luncheon in Taipei, he met Norman Vincent Peale, who asked what he was going to do with his life. Cizik responded that he was torn between joining the diplomatic corps and going to seminary. "Well," Peale told him, "God could use a few good diplomats."

Basically, that turned out to be Cizik's professional path. After seminary in Denver, he made his way to NAE's Washington office, where he has practiced the art of church diplomacy since the Reagan years. This has meant not only representing the association to both Republicans and Democrats, but also moving church leaders steadily and ever so diplomatically to embrace the larger issues of justice within the evangelical tradition.

In 1992, Cizik said he came to realize that the NAE (which was fifty years old that year) had never developed a *public theology*, that is, a clear statement broadly applying the scriptural truths that evangelicals believe to the big ethical issues of our time. Certainly, the movement was clear on its sanctity-of-life issues, but beyond these, the public had no understanding of what the movement was about— of what it means to them, in St. Augustine's phrase, to be citizens "of both heaven and earth."

To define this not only in words but in deeds, he and others began to gradually build bridges of collaboration between evangelicals and other groups. "It struck me that the place to start this campaign for a broader public agenda was on the issue of worldwide religious persecution," he said. Thus, in 1995, the NAE became a U.S. leader in pushing for the religious freedom of Tibetan Buddhists, Hindus, and other oppressed worshippers. Step-by-step, Cizik has helped to move evangelical churches into some surprising political collaborations: with the American Civil Liberties Union on the issue of prison rape, for example, and with feminists on the fight against the sexual trafficking of girls around the world.

So, when he climbed onto the big issue of climate change in 2002, it was not his first rodeo, but it definitely has been his roughest ride. Why? Because this one strikes at the heart of corporate power, big money, and partisan politics. Yet in the context of developing a public theology, it makes perfect sense for evangelicals to take on this issue because the scriptural basis for activism so strongly links the heavenly and the earthly.

Cizik pointed out that while evangelicals are called to address personal sin, "We also need to understand that there is such a thing as corporate sin. And the only way you can address and change what is corporate sin—the potentially self-destructive tendencies of a whole society and our government—is by understanding that we as citizens have to speak out on these structural issues." Applying this thought to climate change, Cizik said, "If people understand that it's a moral issue—not a red state/blue state or even a green issue, but a moral issue—then they will feel *empowered*."

Aha! There you have the reason for the vehemence and the sense of panic behind the attacks on Cizik. It's not him that the Inhofe-Dobson clique really fears. It's an empowered citizenry. If ordinary people, evangelicals as well as greens, begin to sense the immorality of the selfish destructiveness of man-made climate change, then the corporate-political axis that sustains the selfishness is itself imperiled.

This is where Cizik's sting becomes especially terrifying to the old guard, which thought it owned the evangelical movement. And he is not hesitant to apply the sting: "The religious right, in effect, hijacked evangelicalism to a partisan political agenda. We've adopted the agenda of the Republican Party, which is largely serving the interests of the oil and gas and utility industries who pay large donations to Republican politicians. And thus, can we expect that party to speak out on behalf of Creation Care without our political advocacy? Of course not."

For Cizik and the growing number of his allies in the movement, stepping forward on Creation Care is not at all a departure from either principle or history. "We are simply reclaiming the evangelical heritage," he told me, citing the history of evangelical abolitionists who railed against slavery, as well those who marched with the suffrage movement.

On the other hand, he deplores the perversion of the heritage in the 1950s and 1960s, when most evangelicals did not meet the biblical standard for justice, choosing to sit on their hands during the civil rights movement rather than stand for the equality of all people. "They were willing to tolerate the structural sin of racism," he said with a mixture of anger and genuine sadness.

For Cizik, climate change is an overarching issue of justice—the biggest of the twenty-first century—and he is deeply passionate about it. "Unlike our evangelical fathers who sat on their hands and tolerated racism, we will not sit on our hands today, and we will not

"When asked about hell, Jesus used the word 'Gehenna.' He referred to a place outside of Jerusalem that was a garbage heap. This is Jesus's description of hell. A garbage heap. And one of the reasons I'm an advocate of Creation Care is that if you besmirch that creation, if you destroy it, despoil it, turn it into a garbage heap, then how can it reveal the glory of God?"

—Reverend Rich Cizik

either, in the end, have to apologize to our children for doing nothing about what is a threat to the entire biosphere."

It's not an easy path that Cizik has taken, but he is not traveling it alone, and it can be a path of bright promise. Evangelicalism is firmly rooted in the Gospel, but it can be an uplifting gospel of justice that reaches out to the larger world, applies action to belief, and unites people. "We seek the common good for what everybody deserves in this society," Cizik said of his efforts. "And, lo and behold, if you seek that kind of common good for everybody, and not just a privileged standing for yourself, other people identify with that, with the values you ultimately believe as a Christian—which is to love your neighbor as yourself."

A PROGRESSIVE OPPORTUNITY

There is an unfortunate inclination among some progressives to recoil at the idea that they might have anything in common with evangelicals, much less that they should link arms with them. To which we say, "Get over it!"

As our friend Fred Harris, the great populist and former senator from Oklahoma, pointed out, "You can't have a mass movement without the masses." Well . . . here they are.

Stopping both the industrial and the consumer causes of climate change can't just be a wine-and-Brie effort. It's going to take more than Al Gore's movie and the Sierra Club's membership to win this historic confrontation with corporate greedheads and political boneheads—and the emergence of this highly organized, motivated constituency is manna from heaven.

Yes, evangelicals come to the cause from a different starting point than many progressives do. *So what?* Yes, they call it Creation Care rather than environmentalism. *Who cares?* Yes, they wrap their concern in the full panoply of Christian beliefs, symbols, and language. *Why shouldn't they?* Yes, they fervently disagree with progressives on many other issues. *Isn't that their right?*

Besides, you might be surprised at how much common ground evangelicals do share with progressives. For example, on practically every issue of economic justice, they *are* progressive. Why? Because these churches are overwhelming made up of working-class families, many of them low-income or union members or people of color. It's not bankers and bosses who fill those pews, but workaday folks who can and do identify viscerally with the populist Jesus.

The evangelical movement brings not only huge numbers (quite possibly the critical mass needed) and a new energy to this crucial cause, but also a moral message and a storytelling ability that will reach the millions who won't watch a documentary or read an environmental report. Progressives are good at facts and bring a surfeit of sincerity to any issue, but too often we fail to recognize the essential role that imagery plays in politics. As our friend Van Jones likes to remind us, Reverend Martin Luther King didn't stand at the Lincoln memorial in 1963 and say to the masses gathered there, "I have a . . . position paper." No, he had a *dream*, a vision! And he proceeded to tell us the vivid story of that dream—lacing the story with rich biblical imagery, by the way.

Connections for Part Three

From the good food revolution in your own town to the global threat of climate change, the people who are producing positive results are grassroots folks like you. In ways both large and small, personal and political, you can take charge, defying the corporate order to make a better life and a better world. Here is a list of individuals and organizations involved in such work.

The names in the first group are ones we've covered in this part of this book, and the others offer a deep pool of inspiration, information, agitation, and organization to fortify your own activism.

Chez Panisse Foundation
Alice Waters
1517 Shattuck Avenue
Berkeley, CA 94709
Phone: (510) 843-3811
E-mail: info@chezpanisse
    foundation.org
Web Site: www.chezpanisse
    foundation.org

Swanton Berry Farm
Jim Cochran
P.O. Box 308
Davenport, CA 95017
Phone: (831) 469-8804

Web Site: www.swantonberryfarm
    .com

Michael Sligh
Director of Sustainable Agriculture
    Program
Rural Advancement Foundation
    International—USA
P.O. Box 640
Pittsboro, NC 27312
Phone: (919) 932-1697

United Nations Panel on Climate Change
Intergovernmental Panel on Climate Change (IPCC)

E-mail: Contact the IPCC Secretariat at IPCC-Sec@wmo.int
Web Site: www.ipcc.ch

Blue/Green Alliance
Les Leopold, Executive Director
The Public Health Institute
31 W. 15th Street, Suite 601
New York, NY 10011
Phone: (917) 606-0511
E-mail: info@greenlabor.org
Web Site: bluegreenalliance.org

Sierra Club
85 Second Street, 2nd Floor
San Francisco, CA 94105
Phone: (415)-977-5500
Web Site: www.sierraclub.org

United Steelworkers of America
Five Gateway Center
Pittsburgh, PA 15222
Phone: (412)-562-2400
E-mail: webmaster@usw.org
Web Site: www.uswa.org

Dr. Richard Cizik
National Association of Evangelicals
P.O. Box 23269
Washington, DC 20026
Phone: (202)-789-1011
E-mail: info@nae.net
Web Site: www.nae.net

Evangelical Environmental Network
Reverend Jim Ball
4485 Tench Road, Suite 850
Suwanee, GA 30024
Phone: (678) 541-0747
E-mail: een@creationcare.org
Web Site: www.creationcare.org

Eric Chivian, M.D.
Assistant Clinical Professor of Psychiatry
Harvard Medical School
401 Park Drive, 2nd Floor
Boston, MA 02215
Phone: (617) 384-8530
E-mail: eric_chivian@hms.harvard.edu

Dr. E. O. Wilson
Biodiversity Foundation
10190 Telesis Court
San Diego, CA 92121
Phone: (858)-558-0700
E-mail: info@eowilson.org
Web Site: www.eowilson.org

Dr. Joel Hunter
Northland Church
530 Dog Track Road
Longwood, FL 32750
Phone: (407) 949-4000
Web Site: www.northlandchurch.net

Christians for the Mountains
Allen Johnson
Route 1, Box 119-B
Dunmore, WV 24934
Phone: (304) 799-4137
E-mail: allen@christiansforthe mountains.org
Web Site: www.christiansforthe mountains.org

Tri Robinson
Vineyard Boise Church
4950 N. Bradley
Boise, ID 83714
Phone: (208) 377-1477
Web Site: www.vineyardboise.org

Connect with these groups, too:

Appalachian Center for the Economy and the Environment
P.O. Box 507
Lewisburg, WV 24901
Phone: (304) 645-9006
Web Site: www.appalachian-center
  .org

A research, litigation, advocacy, and watchdog organization fighting for sustainable environmental and economic policies in the mountain region. The center has successfully challenged dozens of federal and state actions that favored corporate contamination of the air, water, and land over the needs of the people.

Appalachian Voices
191 Howard Street
Boone, NC 28607
Phone: (828) 262-1500
Toll-free: (877) APP-VOICE
Web Site: www.appvoices.org

This member-based grassroots coalition provides strategies and tools to empower local people to fight air pollution, mountaintop removal, and deforestation.

The Apollo Alliance
1825 K Street, Suite 400
Washington, DC 20006
Phone: (202) 955-5665, ext. 160
Web Site: www.apolloalliance.org

A joint effort by a broad alliance of union, environmental, community, and business organizations to achieve energy independence and economic revitalization for America, based on a massive conversion to renewable energy sources and conservation. With coalitions in nineteen states, the Apollo Alliance is building political partnerships and developing local models to advance this encouraging agenda. The alliance enlists ordinary citizens to be a grassroots lobbying force behind the merged idea of clean energy and good jobs.

Bioneers
Old Lamy School House
6 Cerro Circle
Lamy, NM 87540
Phone: (877) 246-6337
  (877-BIONEER)
E-mail: info@bioneers.org
Web Site: www.bioneers.org

A network of activists, visionaries, businesspeople, and other biological pioneers who create new economic models to unite nature, culture, and spirit. Holds an annual Bioneers conference that brings together scientific and social innovators.

Coal River Mountain Watch
P.O. Box 651
Whitesville, WV 25209
Phone: (304) 854-2182
Web Site: www.crmw.net

Established in 1998 to help West Virginia residents battle the coal giants that are destroying the mountains, the quality of life, and people's health. Also runs "Tending the Commons," a large cultural project that tells the rich stories of the people and the mountains in this region.

GRACE Factory Farm Project
215 Lexington Avenue, Suite 1001
New York, NY 10016
Phone: (212) 726-9161
E-mail: info@factoryfarm.org
Web Site: www.factoryfarm.org

A research, advocacy, and activist organization that works to eliminate factory farms and support sustainable, healthy, and humane food production. Provides organizing and support for community groups that are fighting industrial agriculture. Also maintains an online "Eat Well Guide" to direct consumers to sources of wholesome sustainable foods wherever they live.

Kentuckians for the Commonwealth
P.O. Box 1450
London, KY 40743
Phone: (606) 878-2161
Web Site: www.kftc.org

A social justice organization that organizes, trains, and empowers ordinary Kentuckians. It develops the leadership capabilities of folks, making them a force on coalfield issues, tax fairness, and other matters of public policy. KFTC engages in many creative actions, including taking groups on "witness tours" to see mountaintop removal firsthand.

Local Harvest
220 21st Avenue
Santa Cruz, CA 95062
Phone: (831) 475-8150
Web Site: www.localharvest.org

The best place on the Web to find organic and local food sources anywhere in America. Maintains a nationwide directory of farmers' markets, small farms, and other local retail outlets, urging visitors to bring new sources to the Web site. Also produces a monthly newsletter.

National Farm to School Program
Center for Food & Justice
Occidental College
1600 Campus Road, MS-M1
Los Angeles, CA 90041
Phone: (323) 341-5095
Web Site: www.farmtoschool.org

A collaborative effort by several organizations to foster and spread the use of locally produced foods in school cafeterias, while also involving students in gardening, farm visits, recycling, and so on. Provides information, training, fund-raising resources, and other help for local groups that want to initiate and sustain their own farm-to-school program.

Ohio Valley Environmental Coalition
P.O. Box 6753
Huntington, WV 25773-6753
Phone: (304) 522-0246
E-mail: ohvec@ohvec.org
Web Site: www.ohvec.org

A coalition of regional activists working to protect and improve the environment in the Southern Appalachian Mountains. Focuses on education and on organizing and building coalitions, with a current emphasis on stopping mountaintop removal.

Organic Consumers Association
6771 South Silver Hill Drive
Finland, MN 55603
Phone: (218) 226-4164
Web Site: www.organicconsumers
  .org

A grassroots organization and online advocacy group that is focused specifically on the needs of America's estimated fifty million organic consumers. Maintains an action network of 850,000 members, who take on everything from mad cow disease to Monsanto's "Frankenfoods." Provides a Web-based buying guide of green and organic businesses within twenty miles of your home address.

Research, Education, Action and Policy on Food Group (REAP)
P.O. Box 5632
Madison, WI 53705
Web Site: www.reapfoodgroup.org

A Wisconsin-based organization that connects food producers, consumers, educators, community organizations, and policy makers, assisting them in building regional food systems that are healthy, just, and sustainable. Provides information and materials for various "Buy Local" programs.

Slow Food USA
20 Jay Street, Suite 313
Brooklyn, NY 11201
Phone: (718) 260-8000
Web Site: www.slowfoodusa.org

Helps consumers, restaurateurs, policy makers, and others to see the destructive effects of our industrial food system and to shift toward a sustainable, regional system that is good, clean, fair, and enjoyable. With 140 local chapters in the United States, Slow Food publishes a quarterly newsletter (*The Snail*), holds public forums, and creates food events across the country.

Sojourners
3333 14th Street, NW, Suite 200
Washington, DC 20010
Phone: (202) 328-8842
E-mail: sojourners@sojo.net
Web Site: www.sojo.net

Headed by Reverend Jim Wallis, members of this committed group of Christians work together to live a gospel life that articulates the biblical call to social justice. Publishes *Sojourners* magazine, holds numerous public policy forums, forges partnerships with other faiths, and issues action alerts.

Tikkun Community and the Network of Spiritual Progressives
2342 Shattuck Avenue, #1200
Berkeley, CA 94704
Phone: (510) 644-1200
Web Site: www.tikkun.org

Founded by Rabbi Michael Lerner to create a spiritual vision and voice that offer an alternative to the political right wing and to our society's ethos of selfishness, materialism, and cynicism, Tikkun is an interfaith effort to foster a "politics of meaning." It publishes *TIKKUN* magazine, holds forums with spiritual thinkers and social activists, and generally works to expand and unite the network of spiritual progressives.

Final Thoughts

"It does not require a majority to prevail, but rather an irate, tireless minority keen to set brush fires in people's minds."

—Samuel Adams

C ontrary to the contrived wisdom of the Powers That Be, our purpose on Earth is not to be "good" boys and girls in obedient service to the needs of multinational corporations. It is unnatural, unproductive, and ultimately unfulfilling for our society to consist of people who meekly conform to the corporate order and submit to the soul-crushing list of "don'ts" that our cultural arbiters try to impose on the naturally rebellious spirit of us Americans. "Don't talk back," they hiss at us. "Don't get out of line, don't be different, and— above all—don't question the big-business view of what it means to be a 'success.'"

These dont's add up to a wicked con job on you and me. Today's establishment is saying to ordinary Americans, "Hey, you can't change things, you can't make a difference . . . so don't bother trying." From the very start of our lives (which begin with a spanking from the doctor, just to set the tone), the consistent refrain from our society's power institutions—business, politics, schools, churches, and media—is that we'd best moo along with the rest of the herd and find our places within the social construct that we're given. We are ordered to

Work

Consume

Watch TV

Vote (or not)

Pray

Be quiet

Die

That's what life is, we're told (both by word and example), so apply yourself to it, get what you can from it, and be glad, for you might even "do well"—meaning you get to watch TV on a fifty-three-inch high-definition plasma flat-screen.

On their deathbeds, very few people say, "Darn, why didn't I spend more time at the office?" or "If only I had bought more stuff," or "The thing I want to be remembered for is that I did it *their* way."

That's not us. Way before the deathbed finale, most of us struggle to find some larger purpose in our lives, to seek something more meaningful. When pollsters, sociologists, psychologists, ministers, and philosophers probe beneath the surface to ask people what they actually want in life, invariably the answer is: Happiness! Not five hundred channels, not a promotion to vice president for vinyl siding sales in the Midwest region, not even a million dollars.

What is this happiness? Friends and family, more leisure and learning, more sharing and giving, more laughter, stories, music, nature walks, good food and drink . . . fun. And, yes, work, but work that is meaningful, satisfying, and rewarding, liberating the soul rather than trapping it in an office cubicle or a corporate uniform.

So why not act on what we truly want? Why not opt out of *their* social construct and define for ourselves what it means to live? The ruling powers of today are ruling not so much by the whip, but by an insidious system of self-entrapment, telling us to cling to precarious jobs with our fingertips and to fear losing any meager health coverage we might have. We must do our part for the holy GDP by constantly buying things, even when this puts our families in debt, which we're then chastised for racking up. (After 9/11, when the president was asked what the American people could do, he pointedly advised, "Go shopping.")

Meanwhile, the system does not tell us that within our grasp, there are workable alternatives to this script.

> *(Whoa! Who said alternatives? Alternatives are just frou-frou, flights of fantasy, the domain of misfits, losers, and nutcakes. Alternatives are the detritus of the self-absorbed sixties, the stuff of hippies, the devil's own path to anarchy. Beware of alternativism! Turn away from such thoughts! Get back to work!)*

Sheesh, Limbaugh-breath, you seem to have forgotten something fundamental about our great country: America itself is an alternative!

Start with the numerous native cultures, rich with alternative ways of looking at life, that helped to shape what we are as a nation. Then came European settlers seeking alternatives to the stifling religious and political constrictions in their homelands. The Founders dared to experiment with an alternative political system and a radically different form of government. Africans, ripped from their continent and forced into slavery, nonetheless introduced alternatives in community, politics, food, and music that help to define America today. The huge influx of ethnic immigrants who arrived around 1900, fleeing from the deprivations of the Old Country, delivered alternatives to their new country, ranging from language to the richness of the family-centered "saloon culture." The nineteenth-century populist movement, the abolitionists and the suffragists, the big struggles of the twentieth century for labor, civil rights, women, and the environment—all of these and more were about creating alternatives to the suffocating repression of the status quo.

Now it's your turn to be the alternative. In your business, politics, consumerism, religion, and other aspects of the way you choose to live, you have the power to be your own example. You can make choices to assert the true democratic values of our society against today's forces of greed, which have enthroned the accumulation of personal wealth as America's highest purpose and guiding ethic. By escaping the tentacles of corporate convention, you can live a rich life measured not by money alone, but by your own, more satisfying standards of success . . . which include happiness.

Not that it's easy. As you've seen from the folks in our book, alternative paths have their own potholes. But they also open up exciting and enriching possibilities. And just being able to wriggle free of the traps and fetters of the imperious corporate order is its own joyous reward. So, cut loose a little, dare the dangerous, and take a chance on that glorious, uproarious human spirit that is within each of us.

DeMarco's Reading List

While I'm often asked by friends and family members what books I'm reading in the world of fiction, I'm rarely asked about nonfiction. So, out of a pent-up need to proselytize about the abundance of good works by nonfiction writers, I'm taking this opportunity to pass along just a small list of recommendations. These ten (it was so hard to choose) are a mix of recent and not-so-recent books that have prime space on my bookshelf and that relate to what we have written about in this book.

All of these are available in libraries, so you can "test drive" each one, saving your hard-earned cash for the favorites you want to keep on your shelf. If you can commit to only two, I suggest these:

> *People's History of the United States: 1492–Present*, by Howard Zinn. We all owe a large debt of gratitude to Zinn for bringing our real history back to us and helping to off-set the crap we were taught in high school.

> *The Soul of Capitalism: Opening Paths to a Moral Economy*, by William Greider. Everything I think, believe, and have experienced about economics is here, but Greider says it *so* beautifully.

If you want to hang out with some other fascinating folks who also have powerful stories to tell (and who tell them so well), I suggest the following eight:

Confessions of an Economic Hit Man, by John Perkins. Here are a corporate insider's revelations of how the real world of globalization works. Be warned: his exposé is so revolting, you may need Alka-Seltzer.

Deep Economy: The Wealth of Communities and the Durable Future, by Bill McKibben. This is my most recent acquisition. Don't be put off by the wonkish title. It is a lively book that takes you from his home in Vermont to interesting developments all around the world.

Democratic Promise: The Populist Moment in America, by Lawrence Goodwyn. This book goes far beyond the simpleminded tale of William Jennings Bryan's cartoonish populism to document the real thing. It reveals what the phenomenal grassroots populist movement contributed to our democracy's growth.

The Company We Keep: Reinventing Small Business for People, Community, and Place, by John Abrams. The subtitle says it all. Abrams, himself a small businessman, speaks eloquently from firsthand experience, which makes the book a very good read.

The Disposable American: Layoffs and Their Consequences, by Louis Uchitelle. This book was written by a *New York Times* business reporter who has the guts to tell the brutal story of the effect that downsizing has had on workers and the fabric of our society.

Founding Brothers: The Revolutionary Generation, by Joseph Ellis. This is a human take on the "great men" of America's founding. Ellis is a historian who will move you beyond the stilted portraits in the history books.

Small Is Beautiful: Economics As If People Mattered, by E. F. Schumacher. This book is filled with prescient observations about the "bigger is better" myths. Although it was written in 1973, it is still right on target for today's world (it was even printed on recycled paper).

When Corporations Rule the World, by David C. Korten. Written in 1995, this is a searing indictment of the global system of corporate rule that was just then emerging, foretelling the consequences we now clearly see.

If you like these books, please spread the wealth of information and insight that they contain by recommending them to others. Enjoy!

Index